POET-LIBRARIANS IN THE
LIBRARY OF BABEL

POET-LIBRARIANS IN THE LIBRARY OF BABEL: INNOVATIVE MEDITATIONS ON LIBRARIANSHIP

Shannon Tharp and Sommer Browning
Editors

LIBRARY JUICE PRESS
SACRAMENTO, CA

Published in 2018 by Library Juice Press

Library Juice Press
PO Box 188784
Sacramento CA 95818

http://libraryjuicepress.com

This book is printed on acid-free paper

Library of Congress Cataloging-in-Publication Data

Names: Tharp, Shannon, editor. | Browning, Sommer, editor.
Title: Poet-librarians in the library of Babel : innovative meditations on
    librarianship / edited by Shannon Tharp and Sommer Browning.
Description: Sacramento, California : Library Juice Press, 2018. | Includes
    bibliographical references and index.
Identifiers: LCCN 2017030859 | ISBN 9781634000284 (alk. paper)
Subjects: LCSH: Library science--United States. | Librarians' writings,
    American. | American essays--21st century. | American poetry--21st century.
Classification: LCC Z665.2.U6 P64 2017 | DDC 020.973--dc23
LC record available at https://lccn.loc.gov/2017030859

TABLE OF CONTENTS

Note to the Reader

When we set out to make this anthology we called for experimental essays, creative meditations, non-fiction accounts, and lyrical explorations that challenge, redefine, and widen perspectives on librarianship. We wanted to hear about silence, knowledge, questioning, solitude, information, access, truth, organization, preservation, digitization, memory. We wanted to hear about bookshelves, archives, mildew, the Patriot Act, catalogs, the list goes on. And we wanted to hear about these things from librarians who are poets.

Why librarian-poets? The symmetries and disconnects that occur between the two practices are fascinating, and writing on this subject is largely absent from the landscape of critical librarianship. Poets Amiri Baraka, Robin Blaser, Jorge Luis Borges, Philip Larkin, Audre Lorde, Marianne Moore, Lorine Niedecker, and Jack Spicer all, at some juncture in their lives, worked in a library. As librarians, we sift through information and are surrounded by the written word; as poets, we sift through information and attempt to shape words, make something. In both roles language absolutely matters.

Librarianship employs an array of languages: from the language of scholarly communication to the vocabulary and syntax of computer science; from customer service at the circulation desk to the rhetoric one employs when asking donors for funds; from the language of government in which state-funded institutions must participate to the very modern language of branding. As librarians, we understand language and how it affects. We evolve our words to meet needs, we call ourselves bibliographers only in back rooms, we embrace and promote phrases that the present calls out for:

data literacy, makerspace, data visualization, digital humanities. We understand the language of hybridity, exploration, and creativity, and we allow that language to shape our services, our structures, our outreach. There is so much poetry in librarianship.

When we set out to make this anthology, we did not want to imagine that by the time we finished we'd be living in a country led by a racist, misogynist, homophobic, xenophobic fascist. We find ourselves—as librarians, poets, women, human beings—trying to move forward, through whatever this is, in resistance and revolt. Librarians of all stripes are now tasked with greater responsibility in educating people about information and misinformation, truths and lies, while libraries must continue to provide services that blur and cut across class, ethnicity, and religion. All this while budget cut after budget cut is handed down. If libraries are to continue to provide space and resources for critical reflection, then librarians must critically reflect on where we are, and what, exactly, our place is in a world that's calling into question intelligence, thoughtfulness, dignity, and compassion.

There's a similar line of thought in the answers to questions like Why libraries? Why poetry? There's a chosenness, a coming to, a camaraderie in these endeavors that has nothing to do with money or fame. Why do you work in a library? Well, you can't beat the money. Why do you write poetry? *I want to see my name in lights.* But we digress. Poetry and libraries are spaces inhabited by underdogs who truck in access and knowledge, discovery and investigation, connection and communication—elements of the world that seem to be precariously priceless. Elements we might well be on the verge of losing.

As Borges wrote in "The Library of Babel".

First: The Library exists *ab aeterno.* This truth, whose immediate corollary is the future eternity of the world, cannot be placed in doubt by any reasonable mind. Man, the imperfect librarian, may be the product of chance or of malevolent demiurgi; the universe, with its elegant endowment of shelves, of enigmatical volumes, of inexhaustible stairways...can only be the work of a god.[1]

---

1. Jorge Luis Borges, *Labyrinths: Selected Stories & Other Writings* (New York: New Directions Publishing, 1964), 52.

As we solicited and arranged this anthology's work, Borges' metaphors—human beings as librarians, the universe as a collective library—became less and less metaphorical. Our contributors sent investigations, rearrangements, studies, essays, and re-imaginings about the digital divide, the lost and found box, story time, teenagers, wildness, silence, poetry (among many other subjects). The content of this anthology attempts to make sense of our profession while questioning it, and to us that questioning feels healthy. It feels as though something missing was found.

But what was missing? The understanding that change doesn't occur through simply doing the work as prescribed. That play is necessary. That uncertainty matters and can serve as a guide. So often we're made to feel as though time doesn't allow for uncertainty. As librarians we see administrators embrace the next new, shiny thing—a thing that may well go the way of the 8-track in a few years' time—in order to curry favor with those who apportion libraries' finances. As poets we see humanistic inquiry sidelined in favor of literally anything else; who cares about the life of the mind, or creativity, or art, or the complexity of being human when money's in short supply? Lost amid this bureaucracy and alarm is time. It's not that we don't have time, it's that we're choosing to not make room for it. We're busy quantifying, we're busy reorganizing, we're busy.

In 1931, S.R. Ranganathan wrote: "A library is a collection of books kept for use. Librarianship, then, is connecting a user and a book. Hence the very life of a library is in the personal service given to the people."[2] At the heart of the meaning of connection is a binding or joining together (from Latin *connexionem*). That act of connection is one of great depth and goodwill; it's an act—and an art—of which we never want to lose sight, an act and art we're devoted to carrying forward.

The contributors to *Poet-Librarians in the Library of Babel: Innovative Meditations on Librarianship* work in academic, public, and school libraries across the United States. They live in Alabama, California,

---

2. S.R. Ranganathan, *The Five Laws of Library Science* (London: Edward Goldston Ltd, 1931), 67.

Colorado, New York, Oregon, Pennsylvania, Washington, D.C., and Wyoming. Their job titles are Adult Services Librarian, Cataloger, Collection Development Librarian, Customer Service Specialist, Learning Design Librarian, Processing Archivist, Reference Librarian, Teen Librarian. Their responsibilities are myriad. They write of librarianship as a vocation rather than an occupation. They write of poetry and its necessity, its capacity for allowing imagination into their own lives and the lives of others. We're thrilled to present them and their work, and we hope you're as thrilled in the reading.

Bibliography

Borges, Jorge Luis. *Labyrinths: Selected Stories & Other Writings.* New York, NY: New Directions Publishing, 1964.

Ranganathan, S.R. *The Five Laws of Library Science.* London: Edward Goldston Ltd., 1931.

Chapter 1

CREATING CREATIVITY: ZINES AND TEEN EMPOWERMENT

Jessica Smith

In 2008 I saw Robert Morris's *Untitled*[1] installed at the Museum of Modern Art and immediately sat down to surround myself, as much as I could without alarming the guards, in its mass. Morris collected cast-off thread and tiny scraps of fabric from the Fashion District, and in *Untitled* the scraps of late sixties fashion are clustered on the floor and punctuated by low mirrors that reflect the scraps. The piece takes up most of the room, and most visitors skirt the edges quickly on their way to the next room. To enjoy the piece one has to get down on its level, among the detritus. For me, getting down on the floor and breathing in the smell of discarded fibers was like going home.

I grew up in Alabama, the child of two entrepreneurs. My father worked for a uniform company as a teen and young adult and then, at 30, started his own (rival) uniform company. As a child I enjoyed sorting through all the colors of embroidery thread and the shiny buttons; my own child does this now, too, when he spends time with his grandfather. My mother started a business smocking dresses and rompers for children. One of my earliest memories is

1. Robert Morris, *Untitled* (New York, The Museum of Modern Art, 1968).

of playing on the floor while her sewing machine ran; the drum of that machine is the soundtrack of my youth. My parents worked all the time, which is not to say they were inattentive—they were fairly model parents, and we played around them until we were old enough to help in the work. But running a business breaks down the boundary between home life and work life. All thinking becomes synthetic: how do all the pieces of this business fit together with its employees, its customers, and the family it supports?

My dad never understood how he produced a creative, literary child, but studying literature entails this same kind of synthetic thinking, and running a library extends that skill further. As Librarian at Indian Springs School, an independent boarding/ day school in Alabama, I think about the theoretical curriculum, the curriculum in practice, specific research objectives of both teachers and independent student researchers, programming, what students and faculty might want to access from the library "for fun," what technology they need, etc. Because Indian Springs has a boarding program, the library operates as a public library for a third of the student body and on-campus faculty and their families; the library also contains the media center and the school archives. Librarianship is always a feat of synthesis, and each specific library requires skills from all the "theoretical libraries" one learns about in library school as if they were independent bodies (public, academic, school, special, archives).

Growing up in a family business imparts special knowledge that one doesn't realize other people don't have. Children of doctors have medical books lying around at home (a boon for us as youngsters as we explored the mysterious anatomical drawings) while children of entrepreneurs learn a combination of narcissism and self-sacrifice that says "I can create anything if I work hard enough." Until I became a librarian, I didn't realize that these facts weren't obvious. People didn't know, automatically, that I was an Anansi of synthetic design because I had grown up with models who were constantly forced to "think of everything" to support our family. And not everybody seemed to feel that they could create anything if they worked hard enough—or that they had the right to create anything at all.

I attempt to empower my students, as early as ninth grade, through their research practices, encouraging them to do primary research. At this point, some of the ninth graders produce graduate-level work without even knowing they are doing so. By asking them about their interests and not discouraging them when they see that there's limited previous work in the field, I guide them toward doing that work themselves. Some change topics, but some get that first taste of "What if I did that research?" and are off to the races. For some students, it's a matter of helping them construct claims (thesis statements) that really reflect their original ideas and then reinforcing that their ideas are original. You are unique. Your voice matters. You have something to say. You have to work hard, but you can create anything.

To support this endeavor, I stock the library with small press materials. We only have a few books of poetry and a handful of graphic novels, but those are sections that would be woefully incomplete without small press materials. When libraries depend on third party buyers and Big Five publishers to vet their collections, they can overlook the small presses that are publishing the most vital poetry, contemporary fiction, and graphic novels, genres typically printed in small runs by independent publishers. Empowering the students to think about how their reading and knowledge are constrained by what the Big Five think is profitable, I explain what small presses are, the effect they have on democratizing the voices of literature, and how they expand the definition of literature. I create space for these discussions through programming performances and readings by small press authors and working with the English Department to assign small press materials in the curriculum. Now when students ask about a book like Christian Bök's *Eunoia*[2] (assigned to my Experimental Literature class) or TC Tolbert's and Trace Peterson's *Troubling the Line: Trans and Genderqueer Poetry and*

---

2. Christian Bök, *Eunoia* (Toronto, ON: Coach House Books, 2005).

Poetics[3] (assigned to our Queer Literature and Theory class), there is an opening to talk about how "crazy things like that" only get published by small presses that take the risk, not by big presses that skirt the edges of the mess of human experience, preferring the safe, normal, and profitable route.

Most recently, I've developed a zine collection, largely through the vendors Pioneers Press and Microcosm Press (the latter of which offers subscriptions). After working with teenagers who have very precise interests and issues, I realized that I needed even more specialized materials than small presses offer. Zines fill this need. For example, I had a teen with Crohn's disease who was in and out of the hospital. For her, I ordered *The Perfect Mix Tape Segue #5: Sickness and Health*,[4] which deals with a teenager seeking medical attention for a mysterious disease. I have teenagers who are struggling with depression who neither want to read a full self-help book nor talk to their parents or the school counselor, so for them I ordered Adam Gnade's *The Do-it-Yourself Guide to Fighting the Big Motherfuckin' Sad*.[5] These short zines can be read in one sitting. I don't catalog the zines—they sit on a display table. Students can surreptitiously take what they need, squirrel it away in the stacks, and read it during a free period.

There are some challenges to starting a zine collection. Almost immediately after putting our zines on display, I was called into my boss's office to discuss my poor judgment. I put a book in the library with the word "motherfuckin" in the title (we also have *The Nigger of the Narcissus* but no one complains about that). I don't catalog the books so students can just steal them (This is fine with me. A very expensive zine might cost ten dollars, but if a two-dollar zine goes missing, it indicates to me that a student really needed it. So far, nothing has gone permanently missing, although

3. TC Tolbert and Trace Peterson, eds., *Troubling the Line: Trans and Genderqueer Poetry and Poetics* (Callicoon, NY: Nightboat Books, 2013).

4. Joe Biel, *The Perfect Mix Tape Segue #5: Sickness and Health* (Portland, OR: Microcosm Publishing, 2009).

5. Adam Gnade, *The Do-it-Yourself Guide to Fighting the Big Motherfuckin' Sad* (Lansing, KS: Pioneers Press, 2013).

some materials have circulated for months among friend groups before being returned). And because I don't keep circulation information about the zines, I don't have records of which children might be struggling with which issues (records I am never asked to pull anyway, and the ethics of which are certainly debatable). My arrogance at defending my decision to include zines in the collection was, perhaps, also a result of growing up with parents who thought they could just start businesses.

The benefits of having a zine collection are complicated, but I think they ultimately outweigh the dangers. First, although most teenagers have no idea what a zine is, there's an educational opportunity to talk about different forms of publishing, and for the teenagers who do know what zines are, the collection signals something enticingly rebellious and nonconformist about the library. If we have zines, what other exciting materials might they find in the stacks? Sex education books that don't teach abstinence? Religious materials that are not the Bible? Guides for the genderqueer? Second, once teens have an idea of what a zine is, they see that ordinary people can distribute materials that end up in a library. Maybe their conspiracy theories about Hedwig are publishable (see: *Hedwig Lives!*[6]). The idea of what can be vetted as serious knowledge shifts. Their knowledge, their unique experiences, become important, not just to them but potentially to others. Third, there is the potential to engage with subjects for which no full-sized book exists—like Gnade's work or like Cindy Crabb's *Learning Good Consent*,[7] which is four dollars but can be bought on a sliding scale. If the Rape, Abuse & Incest National Network (RAINN) statistics are correct, at least one in nine female students have been raped by the time they are seniors in high school.[8] Parents and administrators might balk at materials that

---

6. Paul DeGeorge, *Hedwig Lives!* (Lansing, KS: Pioneers Press, 2015).

7. Cindy Crabb, *Learning Good Consent* (Bloomington, IN: Microcosm Publishing, 2008).

8. "Statistics," RAINN, accessed October 22, 2016, https://www.rainn.org/statistics.

discuss how to have safe sex after rape or treat your depression, but statistics indicate that such materials could enrich the lives of a substantial segment of the population. Young people who might not want to talk to adults about their experiences have access to materials (by adults and selected by an adult) that can guide them to safety.

As we become increasingly aware of and sensitive to diversity and one's right to one's own inassimilable identity, standardized high school curricula seem increasingly out of touch. As a college preparatory school, we, like so many others, teach AP history classes according to the College Board's and Educational Testing Service's standards, seeking to prepare our students for college-level classes. We teach AP European History and AP U.S. History in our History program. These courses are, as they are currently prescribed, stories of white male dominance with very little divergence into contributions from non-white males or into the oppression and genocide suffered at the hands of those "victors." Even AP Literature and AP Language can diverge a little more from the patriarchal, heterosexual, white narrative, as the texts taught in those classes can be almost anything as long as the logic of thinking about literature and argument is conveyed. The substance of history as it is taught is deeply flawed and aggressively deletionist. Zines like J. Gerlach's *The Simple History Series* which brings "unrecognized or otherwise mis-told histories to a modern audience of all ages,"[9] and *Firebrands: Portraits from the Americas*, which "is especially . . . for the ones left out of or misrepresented in [textbooks], because they were too brown, too female, too poor, too queer, too uneducated, too disabled, or because they felt or thought too much"[10] round out standardized education. Providing historical and personal narrative zines about resistance movements, counter-narratives, Native Americans, feminism,

9. John Gerlach, *The Simple History Series* (Portland, OR: Microcosm Publishing, 2012).

10. Shaun Slifer and Bec Young, *Firebrands: Portraits from the Americas* (Bloomington, IN: Microcosm Publishing, 2010).

African Americans, LGBTQ, and other secret histories can expand students' high school educations so that they are more prepared, socially, for college and beyond.

Knowing that you're not alone in your struggles and you're not lost to history isn't enough. I want students to know that they can publish their own narratives, too. In many cases we go the official routes, publishing in the school newspaper and local literary compilations for high school students. But the unofficial route could attract readers from a smaller peer group for whom a locally made zine would be most directly relevant. The more local, the more relevant. Our zines stand reads, "Take according to your need / Give according to your ability," to encourage students to make their own zines. Kelsey Pike's *How to Do It* series,[11] which teaches skills like bookbinding and screen printing with minimal materials, and *Stolen Sharpie Revolution: a DIY Resource for Zines and Zine Culture*,[12] a classic text on the history of zines and how to make them, offer advice on how to get started. The copy machine and booklet stapler located a few feet from the zines display beg for the genesis of the next small press.

By providing high school students with alternative narratives and the "means of production," I hope to empower them to take care of themselves, witness others' truths, and tell their own truths to each other. They have the right to start their own presses and publish their own zines from the ground up: they can learn all the tools of the trade, from papermaking to binding, from zines. They can take charge of their own health and feel less isolated with their pain when they borrow zines that they can keep indefinitely and privately. They can share their experiences with their peers and reproduce the cycle of empowerment and empathy for others. Most importantly, they learn that they can create anything, and what they create matters.

---

11. Kelsey Pike, *How to Do It* (Kansas City, MO: Kelsey Pike, 2011).

12. Alex Wrekk, *Stolen Sharpie Revolution: A DIY Resource for Zines and Zine Culture* (Portland, OR: Lunchroom Publishing, 2014).

Bibliography

Biel, Joe. *The Perfect Mix Tape Segue #5: Sickness and Health.* Portland, OR: Microcosm Publishing, 2009.

Bök, Christian. *Eunoia.* Toronto, ON: Coach House Books, 2005.

Crabb, Cindy. *Learning Good Consent.* Bloomington, IN: Microcosm Publishing, 2008.

DeGeorge, Paul. *Hedwig Lives!* Lansing, KS: Pioneers Press, 2015.

Gerlach, John. *The Simple History Series.* Portland, OR: Microcosm Publishing, 2012.

Gnade, Adam. *The Do-it-Yourself Guide to Fighting the Big Motherfuckin' Sad.* Lansing, KS: Pioneers Press, 2013.

Morris, Robert. *Untitled.* New York, The Museum of Modern Art, 1968.

Pike, Kelsey. *How to Do It.* Kansas City, MO: Kelsey Pike, 2011.

Slifer, Shaun, and Bec Young. *Firebrands: Portraits from the Americas.* Bloomington, IN: Microcosm Publishing, 2010.

"Statistics." RAINN. Accessed October 22, 2016. https://www.rainn.org/statistics.

Tolbert, TC and Trace Peterson, eds. *Troubling the Line: Trans and Genderqueer Poetry and Poetics.* Callicoon, NY: Nightboat Books, 2013.

Wrekk, Alex. *Stolen Sharpie Revolution: A DIY Resource for Zines and Zine Culture.* Portland, OR: Lunchroom Publishing, 2014.

25 October 2015 / Brooklyn

Jessica Smith

where the bodies wash up

by water   my life

    Lorraine   white pebble bones

the sun sets in stripes   purple

horizontal crosshatch

black skyline rises vertically   loses contrast

the sky and water black

lights, whitecaps, stars

how our parents grew up,   shimmer

raised us with what they knew

bright big moon rises like

supreme streetlight god

their traumas   death brutality neglect

try to prevent

revisited in smaller doses under duress

in moonlight
the river passing

not quiet

Chapter 2

POETRY AND PUBLIC LIBRARIES: AN ETHOPOETICS

Melissa Eleftherion

In 1986, I was twelve and looking for something to dissolve in, seeking an escape from the tumult of home. I walked to my neighborhood library, the Mapleton branch of the Brooklyn Public Library. I craved something stable, something familiar, and had spent many long afternoons lost in the stacks as a child. I went to the desk and asked a librarian to help me find new books to read. She led me to the children's area and pointed at the Juvenile Fiction. I explained that I had already read them all. What else did she recommend? She insisted that was all there was for me to read and walked away to help someone else. I walked around looking for a book that fit, but all I found were children's books and adult classics. On the way out, I passed the story time room and felt monstrous, like an oversized displaced child. I left the library that day and did not return until I was a junior in college.

That's all it takes. It has been recorded that teen library use drops off between ages thirteen to sixteen. This is a crucial time when teens seek validation from the world for their beliefs, actions, thoughts, and feelings; essentially, teens want to be acknowledged for their unique contributions and for their individuality. Teens can be an asset to libraries yet remain an underserved user group.

———

The library doors open and the teens enter laughing. They shout "We're free! We're free!" Kayli raises her arms in a V, Kandace takes a superhero stance, hands on hips. They throw down their backpacks, fall into empty plastic seats, and chat about *Black Butler.* Alex looks up disdainfully from her pencil drawing—"Sebastian is MINE." They giggle and snap photos of one another, draw on the whiteboard, play songs on their phones. It's Wednesday: we're about to play with melty beads, and we have snacks.

Over the past two and a half years, I've worked with teens to create a space where they are encouraged to hang out, make stuff, eat snacks, meet new friends, and play with various kinds of art materials and technologies. Together, we've created regular weekly programming where gamers, artists, makers, crafters, loafers, and readers alike can come together and share ideas. What's been interesting is seeing the different groups cross-pollinate: e.g. a hardcore gamer who returned to the library for one of our Minecraft programs has become one of my most trusted & long-term teen volunteers; a shy, homeschooled teen who formerly attended our weekly teen book chat has become a dedicated tech-help volunteer, educating himself & learning about various digital technologies from other advanced techie teens in the group, while assisting seniors with their iPads, tablets, laptops, & other personal devices.

As the first Teen Services Librarian at my small rural branch, I had to start from the ground up. There were no local models, few outreach connections, and an anemic budget. Our enthusiastic, dedicated staff was sparse and overwhelmed by lack of management support and persistent understaffing issues. Historically, the library's reputation was mixed. There was positive community support for the library with the passage of a local measure, yet the general attitude was that the library was not a friendly, safe, or fun place to hang out. Library members would often come in, grab a book on hold, and head for the door. At that time, being out in the community meant constant and steadfast library advocacy. People were hesitant to bring their children to story time and certainly didn't see the library as the go-to after school spot for older kids and teens.

Thankfully, staff & stakeholders have supported the need for teen services, even if at first they needed a little convincing: "GAMING IN THE LIBRARY?!" Attending Friends meetings and proposing budget increases for teen services were the launchpads for rebuilding community connections.

With staff and stakeholder support, my first action was to visit local middle and high schools to invite students to join a new teen group where they could suggest ideas for programming, recommend books to purchase for the YA collection, help redesign our new teen space (still forthcoming), and eat free pizza once a month while earning community service credits and building their resumes. The Teen Leadership Council (TLC) has been instrumental in helping to build a core group of teen regulars who feel deeply connected to the library and what we do. One fifteen-year-old TLC member recently visited the library with friends who were goofing off and was overheard telling them to knock it off and show respect for "his place of work." As peer-to-peer learners, teens learn best from one another. Two long-term TLC members, Challie & Michael, formerly had friction and often bickered. A few months into the TLC, they found themselves collaborating on a PowerPoint presentation for a Fandom Trivia program and are now good friends.

It's all about building relationships. Since I live and work in a small town (population around 19,000), my personal and professional lives are pretty integrated. When I'm out riding my bike, I'll be asked random reference questions. I accept friend requests from teens I know from the library, and occasionally I get texts & snaps—to which I actually respond—from teen library folks at odd hours of the night. The library has become a magnet for revolving groups of teen regulars who frequent it because they feel a unique sense of ownership. Fostering these connections is not a nine-to-five gig, and I'm ok with that.

As a teen growing up in Brooklyn in the late '80s and early '90s, there was a dearth of secular resources and services, and absolutely no advocates for teens in my neighborhood. The general vibe was condescending and mistrustful of teens, particularly teens who did not fit the mold, as I did not. Recognizing that a singular positive experience, let alone a lasting influence, can have a significant impact on a teen's life, I feel blessed by the opportunity to work with teens and earn their trust. Being an active voice in the community advocating for teens is integral to the work I do.

Community outreach is vital to teen services, so I often visit local schools to promote various teen library programs. During one such visit, I was invited back to teach poetry for a week as a visiting instructor to freshman and sophomore English classes. Once I got over the anxiety of thinking about standing at the front of a classroom teaching thirty to fifty teens, I created lesson plans using various extant resources and creative writing exercises I culled from *June Jordan's Poetry for the People: A Revolutionary Blueprint*, Michelle Detorie, and Kenneth Koch to name a few. Another invaluable resource was a book titled *Open the Door: How to Excite Young People About Poetry*, a collection of "essays, interviews, and lesson plans" gathered to reflect on ways teachers can "impart the value and joy of poetry to kids."[1] Here, I'll focus on two lessons I taught at a local public charter high school in rural Northern California.

My general plan was to attempt to de-stigmatize poetry by introducing students to poets whose work they could relate to. I compiled a short anthology of poems culled from various texts including *Please Excuse this Poem: 100 New Poets for the Next Generation* (Eds. Lauer & Melnick), *Courage: Daring Poems for Gutsy Girls* (Eds.

---

1. D. Lasky, D. Luxford, and J. Nathan, eds., *Open the Door: How to Excite Young People About Poetry*, McSweeney's, 2013.

Finneyfrock, Nettifee, & McKibbens), & *The Breakbeat Poets: New American Poetry in the Age of Hip-Hop* (Eds. Coval, Lansana, & Marshall), along with work from individual poets like Langston Hughes, Frank O'Hara, Emily Dickinson, and Amiri Baraka.

By opening the initial discussion with the simple question "What is a poem?" I was able to gain some insight into students' knowledge levels and experience with poetry, while "meeting them where they are" and activating their extant understanding of poetry as a concept (scaffolding). We read a few poems aloud from the class anthology and I suggested we begin each class with an open mic[2] in which students were invited to read poems of their own choosing.

Their first assignment was to write a collaborative poem. Each student was given ten minutes to write a line or a word, and when the class was ready, students were given the option of coming up to the board or asking a friend or myself to write it on the board for them. Most of the students chose to write it themselves, adding their words to the long collaborative poem forming line by line. Together, they took turns reading their work aloud and admitted that they had indeed composed a poem.

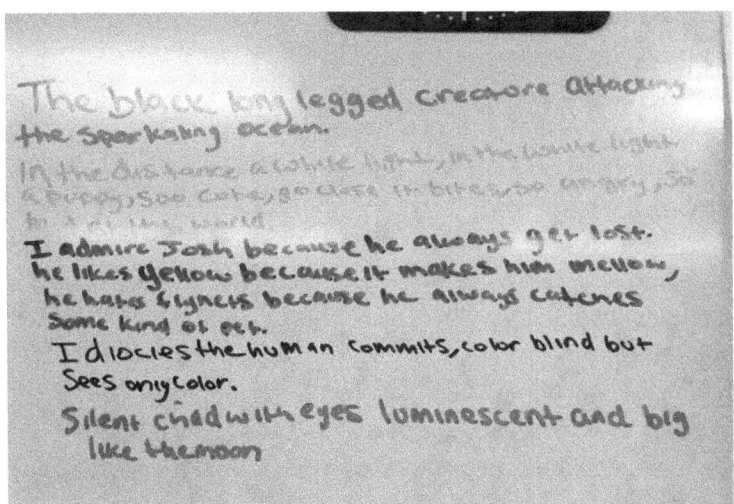

2. Borrowed from Lauren Muller, Poetry for the People instructor & Chair, Interdisciplinary Studies at City College of San Francisco.

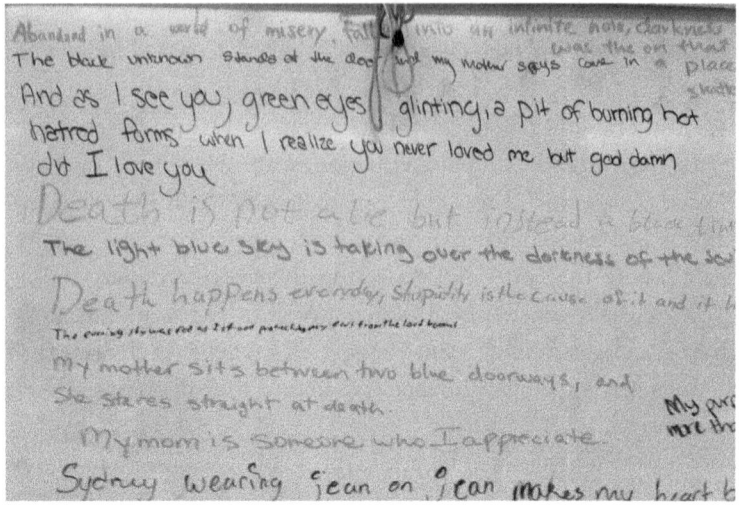

During a lesson on erasures and found poetry later in the week, I led the class on a brief nature hike. The assignment[3] was to choose a poem from the class anthology to erase using natural materials found on our hike. Working in pairs, students were instructed to notice various sounds in their environment and to search for objects in nature to make their chosen poems their own. Getting the class outside and actively searching for mud and sticks and ash to make poems felt very enriching, and it was interesting to observe which students wandered off to ignore the assignment (a handful), and who engaged with the poem (most). One student heaped dirt onto his text and obfuscated words, while another physically taped various elements like leaves and bark to the page. A few students read their poems aloud. After returning to the classroom, we continued the discussion of erasures with a second writing assignment: blackout poems using pages from Ayn Rand's *Anthem*.

Teaching poetry to teens was deeply rewarding to me and felt like a gift. While I think of poetics as a magnet curriculum and often work to integrate poetry and/or creative writing into many

---

3. Adapted from Michelle Detorie, author of *After-Cave* and Coordinator of the Writing Center at Santa Barbara Community College.

programs I plan at the library, it was a joy to focus solely on poetry and delve a bit deeper than one can in a two-hour program.

At the end of my work at the high school in the spring of 2016, I started two new ongoing teen library programs: LOBA, a monthly feature/open mic reading series, and RAWR, a weekly reading, art, & writing club. While LOBA has attracted more adults than teens at present, the core group of teens who frequent RAWR are very dedicated to writing and have allowed me to share a few excerpts:

> You call me gay.
> It bruises my image.
> I should believe in myself, but because of you
> Believing in myself is a mirage so instead
> I feel like an unwanted ewe
> All because of you.
>
> –from "You're a Loser" by Xander Gifford

The taking off of The Mask is a process, one I am always privy to, and desperate to watch and help with. It is very rare I am not there to help her with it. When I cannot we both are irritable and tense. First she takes off the pins that keep flyways in their place. She calls me over, and I place them in the old notches, in the notches made by women before her. They fit as if they were made.

–from "Love" by Alex Rafanan

There's this intersection where poetry meets libraries—a place where fellow residents might feel understood for the first time. One might even say one feels saved by poetry and libraries. I see this among the hardcore teen regulars who feel so strongly connected to the library, especially the ones who feel perpetually outside or othered in daily living. The public library is indeed a place for all— othered, broken, intact, or fractious—and one might say the same of poetry.

Bibliography

Coval, Kevin, Lansana, Quraysh Ali, and Marshall, Nate, eds. *The Breakbeat Poets: New American Poetry in the Age of Hip-Hop.* Chicago, IL: Haymarket Books, 2015.

Finneyfrock, Karen, Nettifee, Mindy, and McKibbens, Rachel, eds. *Courage: Daring Poems for Gutsy Girls.* Los Angeles, CA: Write Bloody Publishing, 2014.

Gifford, Xander. "You're a Loser" (unpublished), 2016.

Lasky, Dorothea, Luxford, Dominic, and Nathan, Jesse, eds. *Open the Door: How to Excite Young People About Poetry.* San Francisco, CA: McSweeney's, 2013.

Lauer, Brett Fletcher, and Melnick, Lynn, eds. *Please Excuse this Poem: 100 New Poets for the Next Generation.* New York, NY: Viking Books for Young Readers, 2015.

Rafanan, Alex. "Love" (unpublished), 2016.

dirt lot

Melissa Eleftherion

feral girl who took to the woods yes we hopped off that bus as it
    left the rotting pit of
Staten Island refuse refusals commerce neon utopia of boredom
    nostalgia i ate it slaked
in mud the rotting garbage patch of my suburban commerce i
    slaked the mud over my
lips a wanting to enter you as the rain fell on your raincoat how you
    laid it down over the
rotting ditch we fucked on the slaking we caked it clawing mud pit
    i left the bus willingly
        as if to feel some kind of love

years and years the news called and green lines gold the perimeter
    a rabbit of time
sounded they had found your body in those woods   what
    was left of your youth then
as four days passed and years and miles of myopia burned the
    residue i fell away

despite the distance my body lies in those woods our haven our
    place   it was mine
too you cannot claim it   you lied   that space was wanting
    and within the wanting
was my body left there in the dictum of my making a blood cull
    from the talons of star
fuselage wrecked atoms of my fueled mist   and now i am
    smoke

you culled me from mud and wilderness i eat it my heart i eat it
    microbiota i salvage it
from the pit of longing that was my teenage wilderness a clawing
    up an errant mouth of
wounds a moth how tender the flaking of its gossamer and fuck
    you wings i slicked you
like the vulnerable pink you were soft tissue and rupture is glisten
    as i move   the
shovel   with my   foot and aim the dirt   for your mouth

bury bury dirt lot utopia bury bury the margins i fucked on that
    line a slit of shimmering
lies

[Previously appeared online at LUNA LUNA:
http://www.lunalunamagazine.com/blog/poetry-by-melissa-eleftherion.]

Chapter 3

Reflections on "Ojos y Orejas are Eyes and Ears" Bilingual Story Time Program

Itza Vilaboy

"Ojos y Orejas are Eyes and Ears" is dedicated to the children
of La Colonia de Eden Gardens and Solana Beach, CA.

As a writer, I spend a lot of time thinking about the reading process.
Where does the reader go? How does the reader make meaning? As a reader,
I spend a lot of time thinking about the writing process. *Where do
the words go? Where does the reader go? How do the words make meaning?
How can I make this little bit of world on the page, how can I shake things
up a bit?* When I am writing, it seems like I have so many rules to
follow, and yet while I am reading, it seems there are so many rules
to break. Writers do not get away with as much as artists do and so
you are very lucky to be an artist. Readers are wonderfully willful
and part of the fun is to play games with them, with meaning,
disrupting the interpretive act.

But as a librarian-in-training, what do I think about? My
internships at several organizations have helped me identify
the different aspects involved in serving any community. Each
organization—Museum of Contemporary Art San Diego; San
Diego City College Library/Learning Resource Center; San Diego

Public Library, Central; Hervey Family Rare Book Room; and the San Diego County Library, Solana Beach Branch—has a mission to serve and respond to the needs of its unique community. The tricky part is interpreting those needs, responding to them, establishing goals, and satisfying those goals in a way that matters to all involved. As a library intern at the San Diego County Library, Solana Beach Branch (SDCL-SB), I synthesize the questions I ask myself as a writer, reader, and librarian when I develop programs that encourage children to adopt playful attitudes toward art, writing, and reading activities.

The Solana Beach Branch is a shared-use library for both the San Diego County Library and the San Dieguito Union High School District. It serves both the students of Earl Warren Middle School and the Solana Beach community. My long-term goal is to be a librarian, so the library staff encourage me to learn new things at my own pace. To gain a larger perspective, one of my colleagues, Ms. Patricia Tirona, Librarian III, suggested I attend board meetings. At my first meeting, I witnessed a group of people openly discuss their hopes and concerns for their community, as well as its needs, including their desire for young children to enter pre-K already comfortable switching between English and Spanish languages. I leaned in to whisper into Ms. Tirona's ear, "I have an idea," I said.

La Colonia de Eden Gardens was founded in the 1920s by Mexican immigrants who were hired to work at the large ranches in adjacent Rancho Santa Fe. The farmers wanted their families to live nearby, at the colony—*La Colonia*. They settled there and raised their children. The first families lived in single-level adobe buildings. Eventually, real estate speculation increased development and interest in the area. There were troubles in the 1980s with gang and drug activity. Local residents brought these issues to the City Council, and along with their own strong community involvement and outreach programs, straightened out the troubles in the neighborhood. In 2010, leading members of the community founded La Colonia de Eden Gardens Foundation to help members of the community make positive choices in their lives, to provide greater resources for residents, and to connect with other community-based organizations.

At my first La Colonia Foundation meeting, I recognized Lisa Montes, a colleague from MiraCosta College. She works in Community Outreach Development, but she is also from La Colonia, from the neighborhood. She recognized me from the Financial Aid Office on campus. I told her about my work at SDCL-SB and that I wanted to get involved in outreach. She asked me to continue attending the meetings, as I might be interested in getting involved in their annual Día de los Muertos Festival held in October in La Colonia Park. I thanked her for the warm welcome, and confirmed I would be there, ideas percolating.

The community is drawn into the side of a hill in the shape of a horseshoe. A main entrance is on one end; the street snakes its way up and down to reveal pockets where homes are built and gardens tended, and then it ends on the other side of the hill to the main street, with a freeway entrance. The homes are brightly decorated with traditional Mexican fixtures and greenery, with an emphasis on the front porch area where family and guests are greeted. It reminds me of my grandmother's neighborhood community in San Ysidro (a five-minute drive to the U.S.-Mexico Border). Her yellow house had a magenta bougainvillea that covered the entire south wall of the garage; it was so striking that, as a child, I imagined it was holding the entire place up like a tree house. The homes are situated within a neighborly distance of each other; you can walk to and from your aunt's house with ease. Stories connect the neighbors, everyone knows each other, and they support each other by making choices as a community.

The "Ojos y Orejas are Eyes and Ears" Bilingual Story Time was inspired by the history and community of the La Colonia de Eden Gardens Community of Solana Beach. The plan: read three to four English and Spanish titles, and to further develop the reading experience, complete a craft activity each time. The craft activity would be a great vehicle to create a "hands on" experience for small children, especially because they are just learning motor skills. I presented my idea to the librarians and I received their (much appreciated) support.

The Youth Librarian helped me to pull popular titles for the program. I developed themes for each scheduled activity. Some of the themes drew attention to caregivers, friends, and family, for example, "Abuelitas/Little Red Riding Hood," "Tías/Trabalenguas (tongue twisters)," and "Amigos (Friends)/Parts of a train." Other themes were related to aspects of storytelling, for example, "Narrative Suspense/The Three Little Pigs/Los Tres Cochinitos," and "Humor/Dr. Seuss/Rhymes in Spanish." All of the crafts were derived from traditional Latin American practices, for example, alebríjes from Oaxaca, molas (origins Kuna) from Panama, and the Aztec codices (origins Nahuatl). When possible, I used titles with both English and Spanish versions. I was attracted to undoing notions of hierarchy between the two languages and so presented them as languages side-by-side. For example, "Wolves" by Emily Gravett (2006) is available in Spanish. I would say, "Lobos," and the kids responded sympathetically to that little rabbit in both versions, all the same. The children moved between the two languages as if on roller skates; they would glide in and out of words, concepts, and ideas, all through play.

The title "Ojos y Orejas are Eyes and Ears" invokes the visual and auditory aspects of the five senses, the ones most readily insisted upon in the reading and writing processes. However, the program also aimed to engage the other senses—touch, taste, and smell. I brought nutritious but delicious snacks. We talked about food. They were proud of all the teeth that had perished in the battle of apples. For the crafts, I made it a point to use different materials each time: tactile and textured, items that would lend traction to the activity. I was probably learning more from the kids than they were learning from me, but I hoped they were having fun. I was terrible at reading; I broke character all the time and laughed along with their bright little faces. It was fun switching from book to book and keeping them on their toes. A caregiver confessed she had never seen her child sit still and focus his attention on one thing long enough to get over the impulse *to give up on the task*. He was also having a tough time handling the age-appropriate scissors. And then it occurred to me—the proverbial anvil that falls on the poor Wily Coyote—the kids are learning how to do things they do not know how to do yet. The kids are learning how to read words they do not know yet. The kids are writing about experiences they have not yet had or never will—unless we reconsider the "panda-dragon-butterfly" or the *dragones con tacones y pelo de palmas y cocos* of the mountains who drag race to get peanut butter and ice cream, according to Simon, age five.

I spent the entire summer reading, writing, and crafting with the children. Parents, caregivers, friends, and neighbors also came out to hang out at the library for an hour or two. Nobody felt that they had to do anything, but they *could* do something. Children are always on the "go" and at the conclusion of every craft activity (the end of the story time), I would ask each one, "What's next?" "Where are you going now?" Usually they were on the way to the store. Each child said this with the calm aplomb of an experienced, licensed driver. Some expressed discontent that they were not going to get toys at the store. But once in awhile, a child would reply he or she was "going home."

Where do readers and writers go when they are reading and writing? They go somewhere. Children go somewhere, too. They learn how to go and to come back, hopefully with stories to tell. Reflecting on my experiences as a writer, reader, and maker of things, I have learned that it is important to identify the start and the end of any given activity. It is important to know how to start something; it is important to learn how to end something, to bring the "thing" to its conclusion, to bring it home. Storytelling is about travelling, connecting, developing, scattering, drawing, and returning to a familiar place, but one which is perhaps forever a little different each time.

To: Nora

Itza Vilaboy

To: Nora

From: Simon

The weekend was really strange, but I haven't yet hermetically
    sealed it in tupperware
containers for easy transport. The Radiohead review was pretty
    much right on, except
that I would have made a bigger deal about the saxophone.

I wish you had been here earlier to see my try to mend a dispirited
    tire to within an
inch of losing everything I've got on file. Exhibition of boring
    male-type destructiveness
as an impy ex once put it. Upset some birds. I feel dispossessed.
    I'm a terrible
mechanic. I'm a very angry god. I don't care how appealing you
    find me. Chary
beauties with nerdy aviator glasses just are, perhaps. It makes sense
    that no one will
ever know about us.

I would say let's meet up for a drink but you know.

Only that I need to hear from you, ice plant.

Why the interest in The Immoralist? Last night I watched Twilight
    Part Deux and read
the Duino Elegies at the same time. Is it possible that both could
    make me feel the
same thing? I must be irreparably broken, but then angels and

vampires do have some
things in common.

Perhaps just as you left it, my porch looks over a park, a modest
    tract with a few elms
and an unceasingly sad menagerie of playground equipment, the
    latter of which have
been ringed around by a hapless pool of sand. The sparrows tell me
    your secrets, the
jacaranda is your bold kimono. We should hang out soon.

Chapter 4

The Weltanschauung of a (Very Particular) Poet-Librarian

Michele R. Santamaria

I.

If I stare at my face long enough in the mirror, it stops making sense. The high indigenous cheekbones, the full lips, the broad nose become one nonsensical blur. As someone who was labeled "exotic" early on, I scrutinize my face frequently in the mirror: to find fault because I've internalized the notion that my nose is "too broad" and to figure out a way to be less visible in a normatively white world. To be less visible or, optimally, to be invisible affords me a great deal of freedom, allows me to be a shapeshifter, someone who can come and go from rooms without being noticed, someone who can change the way she looks simply by taking off her glasses or painting her lips—a different woman depending upon whether I choose bright warrior red or muted posh nude.

To assist with this invisibility strategy, I frequently pull my hair back, sometimes *even* going as far as twisting my thick, otherwise wild hair into the librarian's stereotypical bun. To complete the costume, glasses. Always glasses. In this guise, I was called "mousy" by a neighbor, though I'm not sure if it was my personality or my face that he was reading in this way. It annoyed me at the time, but then I realized that "mousy," or a few notches above "mousy," is what I aim for in my day-to-day life—the hiddenness of that mouse, at least.

II.

"Michele Santamaria" was born in the mountains of Ecuador, and in the mountains of Ecuador being able to hide what you were thinking behind a stoic face was essential to staying alive. The Indians of the highlands, where I was born, survived colonization through a number of means. One of those, which is immortalized in Ecuadorian jokes about their silence and silent faces, is also analyzed in the ethnographic and historical academic literature of the Andes which I have studied as an anthropologist. During the fight for independence, Andean Indians were sometimes "ridden" as horses because horses were not able to traverse many of the mountain passes. To be used in this manner (and many others) as a beast of burden and to not reveal your rage takes practice and discipline. But it also helps somewhat if your face can be shaped into a blank, noncommittal, hidden slate. I have made a thirty-two year commitment to that kind of face since I moved to the States.

None of my background, not the Andean heritage on my father's side nor the Jewish South American lineage from my mother's, has made sense to my colleagues in any of the university libraries in which I've worked. What I mean by this is that one would think academic librarians might know something about Latin America or cultural hybridity, but all indications point to an unequivocal "no." I suppose asking them to know what I know as a Latin American Studies librarian and a Latin American-American is expecting too much. After all, I've spent my entire life learning it. But what bothers me most is their complacency about their level of intercultural competence, especially since it informs their interactions with the rest of the university community. This complacent obliviousness is typified by constant microaggressions that, if challenged, result in focusing on hurt white feelings. And this aligns with the fact that too many white people, who compose 87% of librarianship, believe themselves to be in favor of "diversity" but cannot engage in authentic, day-to-day ways of valuing difference.

To explain any part of my hybrid heritage would require charts, diagrams, perhaps a mini-conference, and, honestly, I don't have the time, patience, or fiscal-spiritual budget for that kind of project. Mostly, I just do my best to avoid the people who are likely to say the most offensive things and when they do I put on my best Andean face, say nothing, and retreat into my office. Simply spending an entire evening explaining South American food to several white academic librarians at a library conference dinner was miserable enough; I had the privilege of becoming their unpaid culinary tour guide. How silly-naïve of me to have volunteered some information about ceviche and then think I would be allowed to eat in peace. The librarian in me wished that saying more about the cuisine would inspire them to learn something deeper about other cultures on their own. But that isn't how official diversity projects actually play out in academia. (Supposed allies show up to diversity and inclusion meetings with the demand that people of color provide reading lists and expertise. Old story. Again and again. Ad infinitum.) The librarian wants to educate, but it is the poet in me who puts on the face, the face that says nothing.

Most explanations about my background, if offered to white Anglos in conversation, are met with glazed eyes. It has only taken me eighteen years to realize that I need to say "Florida" when asked where I'm from and to reserve the rest for poems or creative non-fiction essays. "Michele Santamaria" only exists in the written word and that is probably why "Michele Santamaria" has been writing in earnest since she was seven. It all started with a poem in Spanish comparing my mother's sweetness to that of a candy. While this was definitely corny/cursi even in Spanish, I promise that it works better in a Romance language. Incidentally, that blatant sugarcoated lie-with-a-rhyme-scheme got me a free lunch with my mother and my teacher as well as a bit of time off from school. My older self uses writing to approach essential truths that I am frequently not allowed to speak of in daily life. Though I feel forbidden to speak these truths in my professional life, being a librarian also affords me the ability to more easily protect an inner life.

Thus, in a few senses, I disappear into "Michele Santamaria," a woman with a satisfactorily assimilated name (non-Spanish first name, Spanish last name—like a news anchor) and an English without accent as flat as Midwestern prairies. A name that lands me job interviews when "Eloisa Santamaria," my Ecuadorian grandmother's name, would more often not. Given this reality, the daily physical self I present to the predominantly white Anglo world I inhabit is a costume. Glasses, hair pulled back, sheath dress, acceptably colorful jewelry, nothing too "loud." Because my face, my body, and my mind collude in daily acts of disappearing, I can retreat behind this façade into the real me. Here I am allowed peace, an inner life, the kind of internal quiet I need as a poet and that I've come to think I can only find working in a library.

III.

The woman called "Michele Santamaria" who identifies as a poet-librarian also identifies as a Latina, though her body and face are more likely to be read by the outside world as ambiguously ethnic, leaning toward Asian. She has never been thin; she has been leaner. Since puberty, she has always been curvy, not at all the sort of figure associated with an ascetic librarian.

Many American visual stereotypes about the librarian imply something disciplined and abstemious about the librarian body. A disciplined body is lean. But the impulse to want to know & know & know is omnivorous & somewhat insatiable. Poets might be thin or fat or in-between; I always think of them as hungry. There is the somewhat stereotypical hunger for experience, the sturm und drang of a romantically inclined poet, though I have never done something just for the sake of doing it. Part of this could be ascribed to my reluctance to play out a stereotype. Part of this could be my intrinsically Catholic outlook shaped by childhood visits to basilicas with devout indigenous maids. Such forays resulted in my demand to be baptized at age three. My hunger for experience never outweighed my sense of morality, or less interestingly, my culturally coded Latin American Catholic "good girl-ness."

But it would be an outright lie not to admit that I frequently and very consciously step outside of my body as something interesting is happening—something dramatic or sad or funny or shocking—so I can observe it at a distance even as I am starving to get the details and fire of it right. I am hungry to taste and see, paraphrasing Denise Levertov in her poem *O Taste and See*, the world in its manifold plurality. I am hungry to inscribe it to paper; to get it right even though *right* might not be most people's *true*. And in that impulse towards inscription, there is also an impulse towards permanence amidst the sense of everything being fleeting, amidst the sense that one poet-librarian's life amounts to very little. This is the reason for including "Inscription" as my companion poem to this essay. "Inscription" captures my desire to render the fleeting permanent.

IV.

As I write this and contemplate how frequently I step outside of myself, how often I repress what I would like to be able to say, I begin to fear invisibility. I see this invisibility and stepping away of the self as a way of protecting myself, of being *more* powerful, but it would be untruthful to not acknowledge the cost, how I can find myself untethered from the world—a sardonic and sad spectator, someone or something lurking at the margins.

Maybe there is something of the vampire about poets and librarians—a hunger for knowing and immortality in some form. And also to back away from abstraction and return to the body: a painful, painful, keening type of hunger that makes me wonder what kind of space is left for pleasure. I don't think of myself as hedonistic or abstemious, though I probably lean closer to abstemious if I compare myself to other writers whom I know. I allow myself the most pleasure when it comes to food, another reason why the experience at the South American restaurant with the white Anglo librarians was so painful. I wanted to eat the golden fried plantains in front of me, the slivers of red onion and fish marinated in lime, and enjoy my drink, a Brazilian caipirinha with its lime, sugar, and cachaça—*Oh, I so, so, so wanted to taste and see!*–but instead I sat explaining how ceviche comes to be cooked in the lime or lemon juice over the course of a few hours. I explained in that voice I've grown to hate, that voice of inauthenticity, of librarian, of good girl, of assimilation-poster-child, here to help out with the diversity homework. It was precisely the sort of moment that would have merited that stoicism, that retreat inside of myself, where I am quiet and very, very still.

V.

I've learned that I work in a library because it is the closest physical space to what I would like to create inside of myself, a place where contemplation, details, and the inner world matter. Where, perhaps, hunger doesn't matter for a few moments because the mind is so wholly absorbed that it is at peace with the body and strokes its jagged fur while looking it in the eyes.

I don't think I could aspire to any of this transformative hunger and its temporary satisfactions without having consciously chosen the life of a poet-librarian. The world would be too unsafe, too much for me, without the ability to retreat at times from its overwhelming too-much-ness. And yet the too-much-ness can live and breathe inscribed on the page. "Michele Santamaria" can exist on these pages. "Michele Santamaria" can exist because she is a poet-librarian.

Inscription

Michele R. Santamaria
Epidaurus, Greece

Earlier, we met a man who insisted
Greek had countless terms for love
and seemed to think that we should learn
a few before the bus reached the theater.

Part of me wanted to correct him, explain
we weren't even close acquaintances—
instead, I leaned towards you, as if
you were a younger brother who needed

protecting. We walked the last few miles alone
and found no one to compete for the stage
except two dogs. At times, they edged close;
difficult to know if they intended to lick or bite.

When I stepped upon the platform
and heard my words amplified,
I thought, *how horrible to be this small
and still crave the gods' attention.*

Is that what it's like to be the old man
whom we saw wandering the plaza tonight,
frequently crossing our path,
visible even from our hotel balcony?

This man couldn't stop talking to himself,
at times, ridiculously loud, at others, conspiratorial.
As we walked through town, you pretended
not to see or hear him, smiled at passersby

and stopped speaking. I realized we hardly talked
today, or actually any day since we'd met,
that you, above all, wanted to remain separate,
unknowable. Watching you settle into sleep,

I thought of unwrapping the sheets and kissing
your shoulders, of calling both of us cowards—
not out of revenge, I think. Not out of desire.
But to leave some mark of this day upon you.

Chapter 5

AN OPEN BOOKLIST TO KANYE WEST

Scott Woods

Dear Kanye,

I hope this letter finds you . . . in a better place than you've been. We don't know each other—or rather, you don't know me, and I only know of you—so that might not mean much to you. All cards on the table: we probably wouldn't be friends in real life. It's hard to say, since I know a lot of what you put into the world is for effect, but even having considered that, I'm generally not real close with people who are capable of those kinds of displays. You seem like a dude who's always "on" and I'm a dude who's mostly "off" unless I'm performing, which isn't really being "on," but pretending to be "on." You know, for effect.

Anyhow, regardless of what I may think of some of the stuff that hits the internet or your catalog, I feel like there's something I can offer you at a time like this. No jokes, no pot shots, no judgement; just straight offerings.

When I'm not writing essays and poems about who doesn't like black people, I'm a librarian. I know, I know: you think reading is mad overrated (to put it mildly). And I'll be honest, I'm about to do that shitty thing where someone offers something they do all the time that works for them as though it were a given that it will work for everybody else. I'm going to present some book recommendations that no one can convince me wouldn't act as a salve for your wounds, whatever wounds they might be. That admission is part of what makes people who do things like this annoying: we don't really know who we're talking to, but we do it anyway. I'm totally about to do that, but I'd ask you to bear with me because I'm really, really good at this. Also, I'm a black man who works in the library field, which, statistically speaking, makes me kind of rare. I wouldn't go so far as to say I'm the Kanye of librarianship, but I got a couple of fire mixtapes floating around.

Most importantly, I genuinely think this booklist might speak to you. I tried to pick things that I thought, given a fair shake, you might dig. I won't pretend to know what you're going through and real talk? I'm usually blasting something you did, not trying to figure out why a celebrity is saying something unconventional. A lot of people do that to you already and even the people who are longtime fans are probably 90% wrong. I get that almost no one actually knows you and that it has been difficult for some time to tell who means you well. The curse of celebrity, and all that. I understand how that can be crippling, not knowing people's intentions or ever meeting them on unconditional terms. Not to mention the realization that because you are who you are, that is likely to be the case for the rest of your life. So I'm not at any point trying to unpack what you're dealing with. I don't know, and I recognize that I don't know, and human being to human being, I hope you work it out.

Anyway, here's a list of things that you should think about having someone pick up for you. If you have time, give any of these books ten pages of your time and see if they stick. I think at least one of them might. Be well.

The Hip Hop Wars by Tricia Rose (Civitas Books, 2008)

This one is about hip hop and its effect on society, if such a relationship exists. I think we can both agree that it does, though we might differ on what that looks like. What Rose does here is not only dig into what's wrong, but what hip hop could do right. You took some swings at these questions with *My Beautiful Dark Twisted Fantasy*. This is kind of the thinking behind why swings like that are important. Keep swinging, Ye.

Book of Hours by Kevin Young (Knopf, 2014)

A lot of people speak on your grief like they know it. I think that's unfair to you, but in case there are parts of what you're dealing with related to grief, this is a book you should check out. I'll warn you now: it's poetry, but it's poetry by one of the best cats doing it today. And he isn't dusty with the shit: Kevin Young is about our age, black, and knows his way around the realities of loss, grief, and how to process them through art. He lost his father a while back and he's come back again and again to that reality, unpacking it over multiple books, seemingly unconcerned entirely about the market for what was his necessary work. That's because no one book—or album—can contain it. You should know that there are people at your level (in this case in other fields) who understand that. I imagine the composer of *808s & Heartbreak* might relate to that.

Picasso on Art: A Selection of Views edited by Dore Ashton (Da Capo Press, 1988)

You've mentioned Picasso in relationship to yourself in the past, so let's talk about it. I found those comparisons patently ridiculous, partially because I've read this book. Picasso had a great many insights into every level of the game, but the stuff that really stuck with me was how hard he was on his own work. People would gush at an exhibit and he'd be like—and I quote—"Museums are just a lot of lies, and the people who make art their business are mostly imposters." And every time someone tried to dissect what he was doing with his art he shut them down pretty hard. Not rudely, just anti-intellectually. Someone would ask, "Did you consider this technique over that one?" and Picasso would be like, "Uh, what technique?" You have gangsterism in common with Picasso, but he was the epitome of a fuck-you life. We could all stand to take a little more of that away from Picasso instead of "That drawing is worth a million dollars."

Hamburger America: A State-by-State Guide to 150 Great Burger Joints by George Motz (Running Press, 2011)

I don't know what your diet is like, so feel free to switch this out for something similar, but I'm not recommending it for the nutritional value. I'm recommending it because you should add a passion to your life that isn't tied to anything else you already love or do. We should all keep activities in our lives that are strictly ours, that we can do alone and don't lend themselves to approval in any way. It's about the journey, kind of like collecting vinyl or building model train sets (holler at Rod Stewart about that one. His set is SICK). I once read this series by Lawrence Block (starts with *Hit Man*) about an aging assassin who took on jobs later in his career just so he could keep his new stamp collecting habit going. I'm not suggesting you should take up wetwork, but you should definitely take up something that requires passion to see through, and is just a little past what you know. A tour of hamburger joints across the country in low key or small town establishments was my thing, though I didn't get very far down the list. Take the baton, Kanye!

Mingering Mike: The Amazing Career of an Imaginary Soul Superstar by Dori Hadar (Princeton Architectural Press, 2007)

Imagine digging through a record store's catalog, the used and dusty stuff in the back. Imagine finding some interesting records by this cat named "Mingering Mike" whose album covers suggest he was one of the biggest names in the music business at some point, but you never heard of him and you KNOW music. Imagine finding fifty of those records and 45s, complete with hand drawn covers and liner notes. Imagine that when you check the records for condition, you discover that they're all cardboard—that there are no actual albums—and that every record you found is one of a kind because they were all done by a teenager trying to escape the world around him. And then he disappeared without a trace. Now imagine all of that really happened because it did. This book is mostly pictures of the album covers and "records" ("Mike" drew the grooves on the records, Ye . . . the grooves!) with some story mixed in, so it's a quick burn that you'll definitely relate to. I remember wanting to be famous in high school and making fake album covers. You know, trying to throw that into the universe to see if it would answer. Mingering Mike took that expressive energy to the next level, except he wasn't really making the music. That's some hardcore vision work.

Democracy in Black by Eddie S. Glaude, Jr. (Crown, 2016)

A lot of people would tell you that if you're going to read one book on racism written in the last few years, it should be *The New Jim Crow* by Michelle Alexander. I absolutely agree with that recommendation in most circumstances, but this is my list to you, so I'm suggesting this one. It lays out almost all of the same issues and ideas, but in a form that lets you see how they play out in individual people's lives instead of broad statistics. Glaude puts you in the room with the people in the middle of these true stories, and sometimes we need to see how these things we think we have a grasp on affect real people. Also, if you want to run for president in four years—and apparently that's less unlikely a goal as anyone assumed a year ago—you'll need some on-the-ground anecdotes. Again, you could pick either book and not be wrong, and you should definitely get to both, but my gut tells me you'd dig this one more because of the narrative style.

How Music Works by David Byrne (Canongate Books, 2012)

Former lead singer of the Talking Heads wrote this huge tome about music from historical origins to working in a nightclub to dealing with record labels. You obviously don't need the mechanics here, but consider the last chapter, "Harmonia Mundi," which talks about how sound and music have historically been perceived to affect not only the body, but the universe around us . . . how it might be changing how we perceive reality. Or something like that. It's a bit heady, but the rest of the book you already lived. The last chapter speaks to something you may be experiencing when you create and perform, but may not have considered scientifically. His chapters on the business are eye-opening and you'd probably nod your head in agreement while reading all of that. If you have his phone number, give him a call. Dude is deep.

Frontal Attack, Divide and Conquer, The Fait Accompli and 118 Other Tactics Managers Must Know by Richard Buskirk (Wiley, 1989)

A collection of tactics for dealing with shady people in business, this book has been my go-to for about twenty years for times when I run out of answers and patience with folks, but don't want to just put them on blast (or rather, when I want to, but probably shouldn't). In the age of instant drags, it helps to stop before hitting "send" and consider at least one other option before you go in. This book gives you options to Twitter rants, and in tight bite-size chunks. I want to be buried with this book just in case Hell is as mind-numbingly ridiculous as America is right now.

Erasure by Percival Everett (UPNE, 2001)

Someone who follows me just sighed really hard when they saw this book on the list. That's because this one ends up on a lot of my lists. In my defense, it appears so frequently because it works on a lot of levels. It's real heady stuff, probably the hardest of the books I'm recommending here, but I think the overall message might speak to you. It's about a writer who puts out books that no one wants or understands, and in a fit of conformity (or worse), he writes a hardcore ghetto-ass novel under a pen name that blows up. So now he has to figure out how to navigate the world as someone other than who he is.

Hood Minotaurs

Scott Woods

Evicting him from the library,
Q kicks all of the books, will not walk
in a straight line to the exit,
bobs and weaves all the white gaze
this mausoleum can muster,
laughing into the creases of every frown
making him a nappy minotaur
that's lost its maze. A howling then,
and I do not know if it his despair
playing hard, my despair at the end
of our line of credit drawn scraping dry,
or the siren that, when it arrives,
will pause, wondering which of us
to make extinct.

Chapter 6

You Must Like to Read
Michalle Gould

"You must like to read."

"It must be nice to sit in the library and read all day."

"You must love books."

"Who cares if the library is open or shut? Do you suppose anybody ever comes here for books?"
—Charity Royall, the young untrained librarian in Edith Wharton's *Summer*, to a relative of the library's benefactor

"Library assistants are forced to do everything to books except read them."
—Katherine Lind, the foreign refugee library assistant in Philip Larkin's *A Girl in Winter*

When I applied to library school in 1997, I wrote about monks who spent their entire lives copying out medieval manuscripts that scholars would travel hundreds of miles to read. However, a lack of systematic cataloging and classification meant that it might not actually be possible to locate those books once the scholars arrived. As a poet, I found this sort of futility in the face of the expenditure of immense effort romantic, but to librarians this flies in the face of everything our profession stands for: connecting individuals to the information they need.

Although no librarian would ever get excited about not finding a book for a patron, there is an interesting tension between the classical image of a library that I idealized as pictured in the above story—old and dusty and mysterious, full of secrets waiting to be discovered—and the efficiency and technological facility that are important parts of modern librarianship. It is natural, given the demands of the job, that librarians sometimes express frustration with patrons who seem to imagine us with our feet up and our noses stuck in books all day long, or who think of being a librarian as something anyone who likes reading can do. Sometimes, this may even tempt us to de-emphasize the role that books play in a modern library, to focus on all the other things libraries can do instead.

> ". . . if you decide, yes, I will follow this profession, I will study and devote my energy to the attainment of this . . . career, *you will find*"—he stressed the three words with his pipe—"that an ounce of good business sense, such as you need to run any factory or . . . business, that'll be worth all your Shakespeare and Doctor Samuel Johnson and whateveryoucall . . . three-quarters of your time is taken up by looking out for and clearing up after some crackheaded girl who thinks she's wrapped up a book and sent it to Wigan or Timbuctoo, when all she's actually done is to put it on the shelves where it oughtn't to be."
> —Mr. Anstey, the long-winded head librarian, to Katherine Lind in *A Girl in Winter*

Clearly, these issues go back a long way. There is something quite comical about the de-romanticized version of libraries presented in Edith Wharton's novel *Summer*, first published in 1917, and Philip Larkin's 1947 novel *A Girl in Winter*. I delighted at every quote from Charity and Katherine about how much they hated working in the library, at how Charity's "sense of well-being was intensified by her joy at escaping from the library" and how Katherine could "never enter this mausoleum of a building without a bitter feeling of voluntary degradation." Part of the reason those quotes are so funny (at least to me) is because they stand in contrast to the very real respect, even reverence, that is still generally accorded to libraries as repositories of knowledge within our society, however we might complain about stereotypes of librarians as spending their days reading and shushing people, reflecting a lack of understanding on the part of the public of the wide-ranging duties of the modern librarian.

Ironically, this view of libraries as temples in which every book is holy can make it difficult for librarians to do their jobs. Every few years, scandals erupt when some library is found to have disposed of hundreds or even thousands of books through the weeding process. A quick Google search locates articles about outraged users of the Berkeley Central Library, the Urbana Free Library, the Alameda County Public Library and the Fairfax County Public Library, to name only a few libraries that have seen deaccession projects lead to horror stories in local newspapers.

In *Summer*, Wharton refers unflatteringly to ". . . a library for which no new books had been bought for twenty years," while in *A Girl in Winter*, Larkin describes shelves full of books that were ". . . disordered, upside down, lying on their sides—all beaten by use into a uniform dirty brown." Still, however much librarians explain that nowadays "removing outdated or underused books is a normal part of running a modern library,"[1] such practices can summon a visceral reaction in community members. There is still a feeling that to dispose of a book is a kind of blasphemy.

Indeed, as children, we are trained to think of every loss of a book as a tragedy; we are told the story of the burning of the library of Alexandria, we read *Fahrenheit 451*, we hear the line from Heinrich Heine's play *Almansor*: "Where they burn books, they will also ultimately burn people." As librarians, we host Banned Books weeks and avidly educate our patrons and the public about

---

1. Chris De Benedetti, "Alameda County Library's dumping of books draws criticism," *Mercury News*, January 30, 2015, http://www.mercurynews. com/2015/01/30/alameda-county-librarys-dumping-of-books-draws-criticism/.

the dangers of censorship. But our very work and accomplishments in building this awareness, this feeling that books need defending and that librarians are the warriors that defend them, can lead to a gap between the public's emotional perception of the deaccession process and librarians' view of it as a necessary procedure. There can be a sense of betrayal that arises when librarians don't appear to hold the value of preserving all books as paramount, as the public might expect them to.

> "I remember the first time I realized that books were not unique, like paintings: I was at a birthday party and the birthday boy received as a gift a book I knew was mine; it was on my bookshelf at home, and I insisted it be returned to me. And I remember the birthday boy's mother condescendingly explaining to me that there were many copies of this book extant in the world. I had never heard anything so idiotic or foolish . . ."—from Peter Cameron's *Andorra*

Of course, it is important that we do this work, but I also think it is important not to be too dismissive of the public's emotional response. While making needed changes to our collections, we should be sympathetic and responsive to the concerns and fears that underlie reactions to the weeding process. Perhaps because I am a writer myself, I appreciate that such an intense feeling is attached to physical books, a feeling so intense that people can't bear to throw a book away, no matter how poor its condition. I am even charmed by those who try optimistically to donate ancient encyclopedias and complete runs of *National Geographic* to their local library with the belief that someone somewhere will be able to make use of these materials.

I have published a small-press book of poetry, and WorldCat lists six academic libraries as holding copies. Because the book is small and thin, the spine has no room for the title or even my name; it is hard to imagine what would possess someone to pick it up. Sometimes I wonder how long those copies of my book will stay in the library. When will they come up for circulation review? In ten years? In twenty? How many people will have checked my book out in that time? One? Five? Or even none? What might the library do instead with that slender finger's-width of shelf space? But I don't want my book to be weeded, whatever the library's collection development policy and the benefit to its users of replacing my book with one that might be more in demand. I want my book to stay in that library forever, in the hope that one day someone might stumble across it and decide they have to see what's inside. It may be selfish—it is selfish—but if only one person reads my book in a hundred years, the hundred years the book spent in the library will be well worth it to me.

In her essay in *The Chronicle of Higher Education*, "It's Not Too Late to Save the Stacks," poet-librarian Ann E. Michael illustrates the importance of these sort of random encounters between individuals and books through an anecdote from the poet Stanley Kunitz. According to Kunitz, the act of stumbling across a book of poems by Gerard Manley Hopkins and opening it to the page containing "God's Grandeur" changed Kunitz's life. Of course, one can figuratively "stumble" across a book in an online database, but it doesn't carry with it the same sense of poetry.

"You get paid to do this?"

"I thought everyone in the library was a volunteer."

"Can't you just Google it?"

"The printed page is obsolete. Information isn't bound up anymore, it's an entity. The only reality is virtual. If you're not jacked in, you're not alive."
—Fritz, one of the students in the computer science class in "I Robot, You Jane," episode eight of season one of *Buffy the Vampire Slayer* (1997)

Perhaps one reason that librarians sometimes de-emphasize extant romanticized associations between libraries and books is the fear that if libraries are primarily associated with books, then to some they will appear obsolete. Real and understandable fears underlie our discussions about what libraries are today. On May 14, 2005, an article in the *New York Times*, "College Libraries Set Aside Books in a Digital Age," referenced how the Undergraduate Library at the University of Texas at Austin (where I went to graduate school) moved all of its books to other libraries in its system in order to make room for "software suites" and other instruction centers. This was described as part of a trend in which ". . . as more texts become accessible online, libraries have been moving lesser-used materials to storage." Later, it is mentioned that "Library staff members . . . were taken by surprise when told last month of the conversion, which is how the news first emerged. At a retreat just weeks earlier they had brainstormed ways to improve service and save money. They said they had been promised reassignment after the conversion and feared speaking out publicly at the risk of jeopardizing their jobs."

The fear that librarians and library staff will be left behind by an emphasis on technology is discussed as early as the renowned 1957 movie *Desk Set*, starring Katharine Hepburn as the head librarian of the reference department of the Federal Broadcasting Network. Hepburn's character, Bunny Watson, spars with Spencer Tracy's Richard Sumner, an efficiency expert who the librarians fear is bringing in a computer to replace them. One member of the reference team states, "If we do get canned we won't be the only ones to lose our jobs because of a machine. I understand thousands of people are being replaced by these electronic brains." In response to these types of concerns, many libraries have emphasized their identities as community spaces, adding makerspaces and coffee shops, featuring movie nights and instructional workshops and public speakers. We talk about learning commons and our role as instructors of information literacy. We can at times be defensive about our degrees. Perhaps we can even be overly eager to insist that libraries are more than "just books," as if the idea of books as the focus of a library is a bad thing, a relic of the past that will make people think they don't need us anymore.

"It was your book that started all the trouble, not a computer. Honestly, what is it about them that bothers you so much?"

"The smell."

"Computers don't smell, Rupert."

"I know. Smell is the most powerful trigger to the memory there is. A certain flower or a whiff of smoke can bring up experiences long forgotten. Books smell. Musty and rich. The knowledge gained from a computer, it has no texture, no context, it's there and then it's gone. If it's to last, then the getting of knowledge should be tangible, it should be smelly."

—Jenny Calendar (techno-pagan and computer science teacher) and Rupert Giles (sexy librarian) in the "I Robot, You Jane" episode of *Buffy the Vampire Slayer*

"I had read it long ago. If I read it again now, what would I think? Should I let my memory of it alone? Sometimes it is dangerous to revisit a loved book, especially after a great change in one's life: the book no longer seems perfect; one swears it has been altered or edited, when in fact it is, of course, oneself who has been revised."

—from Peter Cameron's *Andorra*

Muhammad Ridwan Alimuddina is a former journalist living in Indonesia. Alimuddina gave up his career in order to become a traveling librarian, bringing books by boat to children living in the villages and islands of Indonesia's western province of West Sulawesi. Alimuddina's boat carries four thousand books, primarily intended for children, to places that have very little access to any books at all other than the Qur'an.[2] His library has no online component, and it offers no instruction in information literacy, no makerspaces or important guest speakers. But the access to books that this makeshift library offers is at the very heart of what a library is and what, as children, we imagined a library to be.

I sometimes have students come into the library to ask me hopefully if we have access to hard copies of their electronic textbooks. There is something about physically scanning a book,

2. Chad Felix, "Meet Muhammad Ridwan Alimuddina, the Seafaring Librarian," *Melville House*, Oct. 25, 2016, http://www.mhpbooks.com/meet-muhammad-ridwan-alimuddina-the-seafaring-librarian/?platform=hootsuite.

flipping the pages, seeing it spatially, that makes it feel easier to identify and retain important information. Shelves full of books still inspire a sense of magic and wonder, a sense of possibility and romance. We want libraries to change with the times, to grow and evolve to meet the needs of our users. We don't want them to stay stuck in the past like a once-loved book remembered fondly but not re-read. But we also want to remember what was originally the source of libraries' charm for many. There should be nothing shameful or old-fashioned about saying we first wanted to become librarians because we love to read.

Bibliography

Blumenthal, Ralph. "College Libraries Set Aside Books in a Digital Age." *New York Times*, May 14, 2005. http://www.nytimes.com/2005/05/14/education/college-libraries-set-aside-books-in-a-digital-age.html?_r=0.

Cameron, Peter. *Andorra*. New York: Picador, Reprint Edition, 2009.

Chant, Ian. "Books in Dumpsters Spark Debate on Future of Fairfax County, VA Libraries." *Library Journal*, Sept. 25, 2013. http://lj.libraryjournal.com/2013/09/library-services/books-in-dumpsters-spark-debate-on-future-of-fairfax-county-va-libraries/.

De Benedetti, Chris. "Alameda County Library's dumping of books draw criticism." *Mercury News*, January 30, 2015. http://www.mercurynews.com/2015/01/30/alameda-county-librarys-dumping-of-books-draws-criticism/.

Desk Set. Movie. Directed by Walter Lang. 1957. Twentieth Century Fox Film Corporation.

Felix, Chad. "Meet Muhammad Ridwan Alimuddina, the seafaring librarian." *Melville House*, Oct. 25, 2016. http://www.mhpbooks.com/meet-muhammad-ridwan-alimuddina-the-seafaring-librarian/?platform=hootsuite.

Gable, Ashley, and Thomas A. Swyden. "I Robot, You Jane." *Buffy the Vampire Slayer*, season 1, episode 8. Directed by Stephen L. Posey. Aired April 28, 1997. Los Angeles, CA: Mutant Enemy, 1997.

Larkin, Philip. *A Girl in Winter*. London: Faber & Faber, 2005.

Michael, Ann E. "It's Not Too Late to Save the Stacks: Why we still need to keep books in our campus libraries." *Chronicle of Higher Education*, Oct. 19, 2016. http://www.chronicle.com/article/Its-Not-Too-Late-to-Save-the/238106/.

Wharton, Edith. *Summer*. Mineola, NY: Dover Publications, 2006.

How Not to Need Resurrection

Michalle Gould

Children like to play at death –
they hold their breath,
and cross their arms and shut their eyes
until they forget to be dead; then rise
from their nest of pillows and play instead
at being lost or married,
as if their state was mutable, as if, like water
they could flow or freeze or climb without a ladder
into the heavens then drop back down –
they are the first resurrectionists, they alone
understand the trick is *not* to try,
that once you believe in death, you must surely die.

Chapter 7

HOISTING THE DISENFRANCHISED OVER
THE DIGITAL DIVIDE IN SOUTH CENTRAL
LOS ANGELES

Yago S. Cura

I. Hey, Library-Man, Where You From?

I work in a public library in South Central Los Angeles. From
the outside, the library looks like the bunker where Brutalism
took its last stand. It serves mostly working-poor patrons and
their children, so we do a huge circulation of children's books
and DVDs. This neighborhood was an aorta of post WWII
jazz and remained a largely Black neighborhood until the 1990s
when it became an enclave-landing-strip for Central American
immigrants: Guatemalans and Hondurans, alongside the perennial
Mexicans and "Salvis" (El Salvadoreans).[1] "In 1915, the Vernon
Branch of the Los Angeles Public Library was built at a cost of
$35,000 with monies donated by the Carnegie Foundation of New
York City."[2] The Long Beach "Quake of 71" took the old, loyal

1. Hector Tobar, "Latinos Move to South-Central L.A.: Drawn by Low Rents,
They Replace Blacks," *Los Angeles Times*, May 3, 1990, http://articles.latimes.
com/1990-05-03/news /ti-151_1_ south -los-angeles.

2. "A Brief Vernon Branch Library History," Los Angeles Public Library,
October 7, 2016, http://www.lapl.org/branches/vernon/history.

building and turned it into an accordion.[3] But, it is *my* swooping, Brutalist bunker, and it affords me a promontory, and from this promontory I get to create the road as I see it, and that has made all the difference to me as a professional. I choose to grind here because here is where there is the most need, and the least amount of officious politics and bone-headed scrutiny.

There are thirty computers in my branch that are available for patron use (meaning, you get two hours a day with a library account), and a modest computer cart with five padlocked laptops, a digital projector, and a pair of computer speakers from the overstock sale of the Soviet Cosmonaut program. To be sure, as a public library, we try to purvey as much technology as we can, but the costs of updates, troubleshooting, and providing Wi-Fi are cumbersome. The library system I work for deploys a platoon of resourceful IT sentinels to do what they can, but our computers are notoriously slow, and our Wi-Fi signal is temperamental, at best; but, we do provide the only free Wi-Fi signal for miles in this part of the city, although we are a measly four miles from downtown Los Angeles, a city of over four million. On nights I close, my staff and I have to clear the parking lot of all the cars, including those parked in our lot, siphoning our "LAPL-Public" Wi-Fi signal. On nights I close, as I turn south on Central Ave. to catch up with the 110 at Slauson, two or three patrons will cop squats, outside our bunker perimeter, until their video's finished streaming, or that email's been sent.

II. Quizas, We Carry the Wall Adentro

Pinche, puto Trompa you don't have to build a wall because that wall has always been there. And, there are several things we are doing to carry forward this wall. (Maybe, I just used a wall as a device to enter into this dialogue with familiar signifiers, and maybe it's just a divot.) But, it is a very real thing and what it means is that citizens of the U.S., denizens of our inner-cities and rural spaces, may or may not have Internet access depending

---

3. Ibid.

on their salary or level of education. For example, after looking at the 2013 American Community Survey (conducted by the U.S. Census Bureau), the Council of Economic Advisers found that "less than half of households headed by someone who did not graduate high school had a home Internet connection, compared to over 90 percent of households headed by a college graduate."[4] In the last ten years, reliable Internet access has evolved from mid-range luxury to hard-core necessity as more and more companies, organizations, and businesses realize the overhead they can save by moving exclusively to an online environment, forcing customers and people with questions to email their queries.

As we speak, it is nearly impossible to apply for a job without punching keys, filling out some fields, and uploading a resume from a flash drive. I am not saying you have to be Turing to apply for a crappy service job, but if you don't know how to upload your resume, you don't exist, and that scares me because it means the jobs that require the least education are going to be filled by people with too much education, but little financial recourse. There are whole swaths of poor white, black, and brown people in these United States of America who have irregular access to the Internet, and while that might not be egregious, most of the social services that are available to them have migrated completely to online environs where minimal computer maneuvering is not only necessary, but determines your success in applying. The lay computer person will not know how to search an online form for the incorrectly filled field, so that they may proceed to the next screen or page. At my current position, I am prohibited from sitting down with a patron to help them fill in an application for city or county services, because that type of action requires a dedicated person to assist the initiate, and we just don't have the amount of staff that would require. It also puts me in the direct line of fire of that patron's super-personal, sensitive information (with a Social,

---

4. Council of Economic Advisers, "Mapping the Digital Divide," July 2015, accessed October 22, 2016, https://www.whitehouse.gov/sites/default/files/wh_digital_divide_issue_brief.pdf.

D.O.B., address, and phone number there is a good chance I could open a fraudulent credit card account).

Our most computer-illiterate patrons say they don't mind us seeing their information, but I am not sure I want the responsibility of not using their information for nefarious reasons. At my branch, we get the overflow of Inglewood City residents applying for Section 8 housing, and because we purvey the computers it is generally assumed we fill out forms for people. With so much of our public services, education, and work sectors depending on the Internet, I think not having it at home might alienate and disenfranchise one or prove, at the very least, a real obstacle to surviving on public assistance. Think of the millions who have not incurred the necessity of having to maneuver a computer being thrust into our media-rich world of tweets, posts, and comments; think of the dissonance of having to fill out an online application with limited typing prowess (or "autofill") and minimal conceptual understanding of the process to not press the back button; think of all the people that are assed-out of the system simply because they approach a computer as if it were a brick of C4, or an exceedingly tall wall in the middle of an apocalyptic border town.

III. Street Level Bibliographic Information Classes

Last week, I outreached three blocks away at the Los Angeles Ministry Project (L.A.M.P.) site in South Central Los Angeles. It's a non-profit in a poor, immigrant neighborhood, and it serves the community with health and education programming. Many of their clients become my patrons after the school bell, so there were a lot of familiar faces in the crowd. The information session they received from me centered on the library's website, but mostly it centered around the free stuff our library system buys bulk, like subscriptions for online tutoring, online reference in the form of encyclopedias and newspaper archives—standard information fare. I showed them the free online tutoring; I showed them how to renew materials online, and how to request materials remotely. I begged them to come back to the library, even if they owed money, and to talk to my boss who, if the debt hadn't gone to Unique Collections, could possibly work out a payment plan, or process a substantial reduction. I was throwing down my hard sell, so I went for the jugular of respectability and flat out told them they all owned a piece of the library, and that all we ask is that they check the materials "out," before taking them home.

On Wednesday, I held my weekly computer class and only two of my most dedicated students showed up, so I showed them the jobs resources on the library website, and we went to popular job searching sites, futzed around with the website's bells and whistles, and tried putting in different ZIPs for store locations. Regardless of what ZIP we entered, the jobs it was retrieving were almost all in affluent, zoned areas, or servicing entertainment compounds. The only jobs we could find in our South Central zip code were for social workers, Kaiser Execs (Kaisers?), or janitors. I did not have an epiphany per se, just realized how limiting zoning can be in certain areas, remembered my precepts about the dearth of bookstores in inner cities, and kept it pushing. But not before perceiving the anxiety in their eyes as they (sixty-year-old men) eyed the websites for a mnemonic anchor, something that might trigger the muscle memory of having filled out a paper application. If you have never filled out an online application, an online application must appear some sordid juju or *brujeria*. Imagine filling out an application and not understanding that you can hit the Tab button and hopscotch around the interface; imagine if you typed like a chicken with a mangled beak, or did not have the background knowledge to save a picture to a location not the desktop, or didn't know how to attach your resume as a PDF.

Thursday, a couple came in to check the status of their cards. They were telling me they hadn't been in a library in years and were looking for work. Specifically, they wanted to download a paper application for Wal-Mart, and fill it out so they could walk right in and place it in the manager's hand. We searched together for a little bit, but then it dawned on me that most of these stores have kiosks set up where people can apply for their jobs. Whether you believe it or not, filling out an application online sets an economic and computing threshold in terms of an applicant's knowledge. In other words, tough shit if your Internet connection is slow at home or you have no Internet connection at home, and even tougher shit if you can't sit down and type words into all the little boxes ("fields") several times over. I believe these companies know that most of the people coming into the store to apply don't have Internet at home, and don't have the knowhow, patience, or grit required to apply. What else could I possibly do except show them the 658s? If I am prohibited from sitting down with them and making a resume for them, I can at the very least show them copious examples, samples, and iterations so that something sticks and they take that piece of knowhow to their resume and enhance it. I know it's little steps, baby steps, but I can only push as far as my patron will let me, just as the mind will push as far as the brain understands.

Yesterday, I met with an admin and Sister Kathy from L.A.M.P. and we mapped out a four-week course for computer *principiantes* or initiates in Spanish. We were excited because there weren't nearly enough programs for adults, and this curriculum was specifically targeting the mothers, teaching them how to operate, maintain, and utilize a recent donation of laptop computers they had received from an aerospace company. And then around seven at night, an hour before we close, I was speaking with one of our regulars, a mother with two kids, who was helping her kindergartener with her alphabet while her seven year old used the table as a humping post, and we got to talking about the advantages of having an Internet connection at home, and how it was not a luxury anymore seeing as the menu of things available through the Internet had drastically changed.

IV. *Mi Esquadron de Viejitos* (My Squadron of Seniors)

In November of last year, the Los Angeles County Board of Supervisors "voted . . . to push for affordable high-speed Internet access for Los Angeles County seniors, low-income residents and people with disabilities."[5] It's been almost a year since the Board of Supervisors approved, unanimously, "to establish a comprehensive Lifeline program that lowers the cost of broadband and enhances overall digital literacy among disadvantaged communities," and I have seen absolutely zero progress on the ground in terms of local promotions, community investment, and resident buy-in.[6] I don't actually hoist *viejitos* over the Digital Divide in South Central Los Angeles, but I have been teaching a *clase de computación*, or "Computer Class," at my branch for over a year and I've learned a couple of things about teaching older patrons how to use computers, and why that is so significant in the digital desert of South Central Los Angeles.

First off, two rules (the only two rules):

1. The only way you are going to break this computer is if you throw it through the window. (*La unica manera que vas a romper esta máquina es si la tiras por la ventana.*)

2. The digital environment extends past the parameters of your monitor. (*El ambiente digital existe afuera de los parametros de su pantalla.*)

I tell them the first rule so they stop treating the computer like a package of C4, like some dangerous animal they don't want to stir from sleep; I tell them the second rule so they understand that a webpage is longer and wider and more complex than what is displayed in real-time on their monitor. I would like to say that my efforts are helping digitally socialize seniors, but I don't require students to matriculate so it is nearly impossible for me to put them in cohorts, which makes it increasingly difficult to have curriculum ready for my one hour a week class. On top of that, my students come in knowing different things about the computers: on one side of the spectrum are seniors who want to open a Facebook account because they'd like to see pictures of their grandkids, on the other side are seniors who can't access their Gmail accounts and think

5. Matt Hamilton, "L.A. County backs plan to ensure Internet access for seniors and the poor," *Los Angeles Times*, November 27, 2015, http://www.latimes.com / local/california/la-me-county-inter net-20151127-story.html.

6. Ibid.

that I know their password because I am the dude with a laminated badge dangling from a yellow Los-Angeles-Public-Library-lanyard.

Moreover, young people have absolutely no interest in helping their parents and grandparents navigate the Internet; Senior Citizens and parents get cock-blocked from the Internet because their kids and grandkids don't want them on the Internet rooting about, reminding them the glamour of their Internet life is incongruent with that of their pedestrian meh (ennui). I would even venture that there is a direct relation between the computer illiteracy of the parent, and the creepiness, treachery, and troll-like behavior exhibited by their progeny on the Internet. The Internet is an arena that is inhospitable to seniors because it does not look backwards and has a murderous learning curve, but what if we need seniors on the Internet the most? Surely, their spectrum of life experience can prove useful when using a tool like the Internet, which seems to move in and out of focus (mostly without our knowledge) like a simultaneously granular and telescopic telephoto lens.

I do the class entirely in Spanish, and simultaneously in Spanish and English if English-only patrons shows up for class. And, I tell my students that if they only come to this one-hour computer class once a week there is no way they are going to overcome their inexperience on the computer. But, many of them have entrenched lives of have-to; they'd like to learn enough about computers to partake of the narrative their families are constructing on the Internet, but have little curiosity about the Internet outside of those narratives. I think the good fight with seniors is tapping into their curiosity for the Internet as a historical scalpel that will allow them to find images, sounds, and primary texts that elicit the people they used to be, or the places they used to frequent. The next time you are feeling depressed about the Internet, show a senior the Google Maps "Street View" of their first house, or their old street address (or village for that matter). However, it will take sufficient effort for seniors, who have never used the Internet, to see the Internet's value as a register, repository, and oracle; and, seniors fear the Internet's totality as an agent of identity theft and inscriber of names almost to an illogical extent (unless of course you follow the news and realize the NSA's reach). If nothing else, I know we can teach some *viejitos* to enlist in autopay so they can keep cool in their homes and forego having to stand in that ridiculous sun on Central Avenue, waiting for the DWP/Gas Company office to open so they can pay their electricity bill in person.

V. Investing en la Nave Nodriza

I don't use my branch's Wi-Fi signal to actually post pics from the branch's programs (Instagram, Facebook); I know that when I get home I can upload them in seconds on my personal, established, and trusted Wi-Fi connection. So, here I am writing about the lack of high-speed Internet in the inner-city, and I don't even use my work site's inner-city Wi-Fi signal because it's capricious and I don't have the patience (or more exactly, I need the patience for my patrons). I could contact the IT Department and ask them for the password for the secure and established branch Wi-Fi connection, but the request might entail talking to several bureaucrats and open me up to liability as a person with the branch's Wi-Fi password. For me, the route to high speed Internet is maybe delayed until I get home, but what of the people in the inner city who don't have that option? According to the *Los Angeles Times*, "In recent months, commissioners (L.A. County) have publicly committed to restructuring the program (Lifeline) and focus[ing] on access to broadband, calling it 'essential to participation in modern society.'"[7] But how can we expect participation when "13% of adults have smartphone but no home broadband" and "63% of newcomers would need someone to help [them]" to use a computer.[8]

Maybe the problem is that we've already allowed historical inequalities in education to pervade arenas of technology. According to a July 2015 issue brief, "Mapping the Digital Divide,"

---

7. Ibid.

8. Lee Rainie, "Digital Divides 2016," (keynote address at the Internet Governance Forum. Power Point Slides), October 22, 2016, http://www.pewInternet.org/2016/07/14/digital-divides-2016.

authored by the Council of Economic Advisers associated with the White House, "less than half of household headed by someone who did not graduate high school had a home Internet connection."[9] Most of the problems in my country that have to do with Race are disguised as the quixotic limestone of Class. I've been to West Virginia; I've seen just as many poor, white folks as poor black and brown ones; I know the picture of who is poor changes as you exit the cities and enter our villages; but at the very least, let us refrain from more walls until we address the ones that presently threaten our experimental democracy. This Digital Divide threatens to tear our country deeper into its two-class binary, "between a prospering college-educated elite of lawyers and doctors and bankers and a struggling mass of fast-food workers and security guards and nannies."[10] The Digital Divide is important not only because of what it doesn't give the working-poor, but because of the opportunity it affords our country in terms of education and training. By overcoming this technological disparity, we can begin to enrich and improve the skills the working poor can rely on to maintain gainful employment, and welcome back people we have historically pushed to the margins.

The 'hood needs Wi-Fi more than malls need Wi-Fi, but typically malls are zoned in areas that have infrastructure for high speed Internet and thus it is cheaper, safer, and more reasonable to ensure Wi-Fi at a mall than the 'hood. However, the mall needs Wi-Fi more than the 'hood for one single reason: Wi-Fi and technological capabilities are part of the lease agreement. Wi-Fi is a requirement of these businesses doing business at the mall. The 'hood needs Wi-Fi more than malls because accessing the Internet from home is fast becoming "essential to participation in modern society" and we stand to alienate and disenfranchise a whole new

---

9. Council of Economic Advisers, "Mapping the Digital Divide."

10. Binyamin Appelbaum, "Why are Politicians So Obsessed With Manufacturing?" *New York Times Magazine*, October 4, 2016, http://www.nytimes.com/2016/10/09/magazine/why-are-politicians-so-obsessed-with-manufacturing.html?_r=0.

generation of the working poor.[11] The 'hood needs Wi-Fi more than malls because the 'hood needs access to online applications for social services, synchronous online tutoring, online application employment systems, and digital blackboards. If a third-grade class comes into my branch, I should be able to count on the same educational technology that exists in more affluent areas to show them perhaps the route synapses take in the brain, or the evolutionary arc of lemurs—there should be no divide between the way technology allows us to comprehend a subject through innovative interfacing, and the exertion of that technology through its bandwidth. The "buffering" Wi-Fi signal at my branch shouldn't be allowed to define the educational experience of learning about something of interest, like astronomical units or the historic price of gold in the U.S.

Forget that Wi-Fi is becoming a universal human right, the students in the 'hood have earned the privilege of using Wi-Fi as a measly corrective for the years of neglect and half-hearted initiatives that public school systems in the 'hood have forced its constituents to endure. Applications, software, and tutorials exist online and are free and can make tremendous strides in ensuring proficiency, but most of the homes do not have the budget for Wi-Fi, most barely have enough for a chunk of hardware, outside of expensive cellular phones. I believe that the library is a powerful corrective and helps to minimize the divide between the working poor who have a desktop, and those who don't even own a tablet. Monday through Thursday from 2:30-5:30 my branch whips out five padlocked laptops and a large color printer; we allow all the students to print ten sheets for free, and the cybernaut even helps you jump on Word or Google Docs to print your essay. But, that's just three hours a day, and unfortunately not nearly enough time to gain much familiarity, although it does help to lessen the divide. Also, as you well know, slower download speeds mean that amenities and features in video and music software and hardware load slower; it

---

11. Matt Hamilton, "L.A. County backs plan to ensure Internet access for seniors and the poor."

means minutes versus seconds, and interruptions because a stream needs to buffer, or an update needs to work at a specific speed. Could you imagine powering the 2016 "cloud" version of InDesign on a dial-up modem, or connecting to Adobe with a dial-up when you could be using fiber-optic cable? What about viewing a video on "Frontiers of Biomedical Engineering" with W. Mark Saltzman on the Open Yale Courses with an inadequate download speed so that it buffers for minutes right before all the juicy case studies?[12]

I believe the City of Los Angeles should continue to vigorously develop municipal broadband networks. Despite recent legal turmoil, "Municipal wireless networks are cheaper to build than cable or fiber-optic networks and are easier to deploy."[13] According to the Los Angeles County Board of Supervisors "There are other contributors to the Digital Divide. In some rural regions, including areas in San Bernardino and Kern counties, cable companies have not completed the costly job of installing cable lines that reach all communities. In other regions, the cable lines are outdated and do not provide reliable high-speed service".[14] If the cable companies want to drain the last penny from their crumbling infrastructure by having the working poor pay for inferior service, then why shouldn't under-represented communities have the option of municipal broadband? Moreover, there might be a precedent, some kind of historical example that justifies municipal broadband networks:

> Jim Baller, a lawyer in Washington who represents local governments in utility issues likens the modern wireless movement to the rural electrification movement of the late 1800's. Then, communities

---

12. W. Mark Saltzman, "Frontiers of Biomedical Engineering," *Open Yale Courses*, October 7, 2016, http://oyc.yale.edu/biomedical-engineering.

13. Tim Gnatek, "Switchboard in the Sky," *New York Times*, May 3, 2006, http://www.nytimes.com/2006/05/03/technology/techspecial3/03utility.html?_r=0.

14. Meg James, "Charter merger may hinge on whether it can make the Internet affordable to more people," *Los Angeles Times*, March 15, 2016, http://www.latimes.com/entertainment/envelope/cotown/la-et-ct-digital-divide-charter-merger-20160310-story.html.

beyond the reach of the electric companies took control of their electric futures and struck out with their own plans.[15]

You should be here at the Vernon Branch after the local schools let out; the printer is humming out Googled jpegs of tectonic plates, the San Capistrano Mission, Selena, *la Virgen de Guada,* or the Mars Rover *Curiosity.* The chatter of middle schoolers playing chess mingles with the exuberant collaboration of high schoolers grinding out their history project on the Chicano Moratorium; the alcoves in our children's section become tiny aquariums of murmuring as the parents and volunteer readers drone sentences out to the children they're reading to. My library branch sounds like a library branch should sound: loud, but not boisterous, like a nest of bees thinking about starting a colony. Public libraries might be our last hope for exorcising our historical demons of inequality.

VI. Poetry, Access: Digital Divots

So, what are the dangers of not facilitating access to the Internet for the disenfranchised and destitute? To what extent are the people who don't traditionally read poetry being completely left out of the Poetry picture simply because they are victims of the Digital Divide? I guess that depends upon whether my talk of two Americas makes you cringe, or provides food for thought. If you are of the opinion that educational resources are the same regardless of the neighborhood, then most of what I've written here today will likely seem like bunkum buoyed by inflammatory conjecture; but if you have worked in the inner-city or know someone who works in the inner-city, then you understand that the intersection between education, technology, and access is not always transparent in the inner-city. Indeed, according to the Poetry Foundation's report on Poetry and New Media, "The primary difference in the ability

---

15. Tim Gnatek, "Switchboard in the Sky," *New York Times,* May 3, 2006, http://www.nytimes.com/2006/05/03/technology/techspecial3/03utility.html?_r=0.

to access and engage with poetry between our U.S. president's children and an inner-city child of any race lies in the community's social and educational resources."[16]

Inner-city children of any race (white, Latino, African-American) in the U.S. are educated in a sub-standard manner with sub-standard resources and can rely on nominal opportunities to acculturate and become educated outside of the arenas presented by their public school. In the inner-city there are no bookstores, aside from Christian ones (and thus, very limiting), and no venues which stimulate the love and practice of reading outside of the library; this type of landscape sends a very pointed message to our inner-city children. It says: you can read books (of poetry, astronomy, or anthropology) but you can't own any. In this way, our National Combine of Poverty ensures that inner-city children will always be able to participate in, but never own a piece of the Culture. Poetry is important as a cultural commodity because it not only transmits culture, it also teaches readers (and thus, writers) to "engage with difficulty creatively," and to make predictions and connections based on aftertastes in the text, while at the same time allowing, and simultaneously correcting, for mistakes in analysis, discursive U-turns, and repositionings of speculation in lieu of variable "facts."[17] Poetry learns while it learns the reader. It forces us to read with care, but reading is unpopular and has been fetishized as a refuge for the bookish instead of a mental exercise since the Victorian Era. However, we can strive to position Poetry as a challenge that we use to polish our abilities to speak our minds using other people's words (and phrases and stories)

The challenge before us now has specifically to do with access, and the dangers of not being egalitarian in the face of historical disparities. Whether it's access to the Internet in working-class areas of our cities or access to poetry resources, the song remains

---

16. Michael Coller, et al., "Poetry and New Media: A Users' Guide," *The Poetry Foundation*, 2009, accessed November 4, 2016, https://www.poetryfoundation.org/uploads/documents/Poetry_and_New_Media.pdf.

17. Ibid.

the same: without adequate access our best efforts at enculturation, education, and democracy will remain largely defunct.

Postscript: In this essay, I depict the technology situation at the Vernon as it was when I first started writing this in 2016. The technology situation has since changed considerably; after the writing of this essay, the Vernon increased the bandwidth for its patrons. While certain conditions in South Central haven't changed, Los Angeles Public Library has made strides in increasing the technology in all of its branches.

Bibliography

Appelbaum, Binyamin. "Why Are Politicians So Obsessed With Manufacturing?" *New York Times Magazine*, October 4, 2016. http://www.nytimes.com/2016/10/09/magazine/ why-are-politicians-so-obsessed-with-manufacturing. html?_r=0.

"A Brief Vernon Branch Library History." Los Angeles Public Library, October 7, 2016. http://www.lapl.org/branches/ vernon/history.

Coller, Michael, Wyn Cooper, Rita Dove, Cornelius Eady, David Fenza, Kate Gale, Kimiko Hahn, Lewis Hyde, Fiona McCrae, Robert Pinsky, Claudia Rankine, Alberto Ríos, Don Selby, Rick Stevens, Jennifer Urban, and Monica Youn. "Poetry and New Media: A Users' Guide." *The Poetry Foundation*, 2009. Accessed November 4, 2016. https://www.poetryfoundation.org/uploads/documents/ Poetry_and_New_Media.pdf.

Council of Economic Advisers. "Mapping the Digital Divide."
July 2015. Accessed October 22, 2016. https://www.
whitehouse.gov/sites/default/files/wh_digital_divide_
issue_brief.pdf.

Gnatek, Tim. "Switchboard in the Sky." *New York Times*, May 3,
2006. http://www.nytimes.com/2006/05/03/technology/
techspecial3/03utility.html.

Hamilton, Matt. "L.A. County backs plan to ensure Internet
access for seniors and the poor." *Los Angeles Times*,
November 27, 2015. http://www.latimes.com/local/
california/la-me-county-Internet-20151127-story.html.

James, Meg. "Charter merger may hinge on whether it can make
the Internet affordable to more people." *Los Angeles Times*,
March 15, 2016. http://www.latimes.com/entertainment/
envel ope /cotown/la-et-ct-digital-divide-charter-merger-
20160310-story.html.

Rainie, Lee. "Digital Divides 2016."(Keynote address at
the Internet Governance Forum. Power Point
Slides) October 22, 2016. http://www.pewInternet.
org/2016/07/14/digital-divides-2016.

Saltzman, W. Mark. "Frontiers of Biomedical Engineering."
Open Yale Courses. October 7, 2016. http://oyc.yale.edu/
biomedical-engineering.

Tobar, Hector. "Latinos Move to South-Central L.A.: Drawn by
Low Rents, They Replace Blacks." *Los Angeles Times*, May
03, 1990. http://articles.latimes.com/1990-05-03/news /
ti-151_1_ south -los-angeles.

Exposition, Line

Yago S. Cura

At this hour from the Culver City platform
the Exposition Rider, or Ex-Po, hurls east, unleashed,
at untoward velocity to catch this morning's pedigree.

The Hollywood Hills, backlit, effulgent fissures (those bitches!).
Looking south, the crest of Monstrohill at Hahn Park: slurry
and fuzzy. You can barely make out the wide stairway, and stubble

envelopes hikers resisting the grade of another aerobic morning
versus challenge-landscape. You can clearly make out the lookout
    kiosk,
though: all sleek window-pane to induce sweeping panoramic
    coronaries.

Then, past humpback canvases, sound lots and production domes
fashion wholesalers, ginormous fábricas, keg distributors, lumber
    bivouacs
auto body rebel bases, Hydroponic Universities, Trucking-School
    Laboratories.

Past squat orange Tire Churches, mutant trees, and desolate lots
city-block long Jetro's Cash and Carry Restaurant Depot, that
    bazaar
of surly wholesale associates, past gangs of power lines, spray
    painted fronds

and telephone switch centers, past cupcake nuclear homes painted
    powder
peach, and chained to palm trees with blown-back heads. Still
    farther,
as we come up on La Cienaga, her enormous storage citadels and
    overhangs—

her underpasses and over-mergings, we come up on a colicky
    boulevard.
La Cienaga, as she unfurls her metallic overbite, an undertow of
    Commerce
Way back in the background, the file and rank of Westwood
    skyscrapers.

The Sandstone Rome of U.C.L.A., cursed beyond more ridges and
    ranges,
and if you look through the trees you can barely make out a tiny
    Hollywood sign,
or at least the tract in the loam of the promontory where that idiot
    beacon bleeds all night.

Past the Farmdale stop, past the Hail Mary Academic Academies,
the knowledge homes of Dorsey High, and on to the dilapidated
    alleys,
peppered streets that go from industrial to residential to personal
    homesteads.

Past Crenshaw, past the County Probation Depot, past neat
    chateaus
and former starter homes, past stark corners, West Angeles
    Cathedral,
its stained-glass knave, crescent auditorium, humongous semicircle
    self.

And now, Jefferson becomes corrugated outposts, amnesiatic, real
    talk
brick stretches, hardware barracks, and roofing stores until you hit
    Western
and Foshay, Home of the Panthers, and mini-Craftsmen with
    sagging
eaves and feral clusters of lavender and bougainvillea. Then, two
    miles east

until Vermont. On Vermont, Ex-Po creeps across the Jesse Brewer
    Homeless Person's Park
and the Museum of Natural History, the City Rose Garden, and
    burial place

of our Challenger. And for a good ten minutes, the landscape is
    private terra-cotta;
the view is svelte blond women jogging towards their Life Coaches,
    and marauding
brunettes from the Land that La Crosse Forgot torching honor
    discount cards.

But, not before the Expo Rider goes underground, and I get to
    photocopy my face
in the toner of a makeshift mirror that exaggerates my wrinkles,
    platinumizes my smile,
my wry signature, wattage of my inclination to tonic the harshness
    or debark.

Not until the Expo Line emerges around 25th St. does one feel
    spry
again because the 110 is there to compare to your lot, and you
    decide congestion
of cars is like Chinese Water Drop Torture because of the
    cumulative thrust

of annoyances and little rudenesses we wield pre-emptively behind
    our burbujas
and so by 23rd Street we see the St. Vincent de Paul Church, it's
    shell sweating
with cerulean blue condensation, it's baroque stucco flourishes,
    devilish and inflected.

Past the pea green Trade Tech walls and its many bays, docks, and
    referees of labor.

Past the lunch trucks with intermittent neon signs that flash tortas,
tlayudas, and tacos.
Past the murals of grossly muscular Marines, world peace, and
alloy kindergarteners.

Until you see a concrete fin that gives rise to the girth of the
Convention Center
and the Staples Center, two albino elephants of wide load renown,
one ancient-looking
with glass grid of teeth, one modern with uneven bows, sweeping
facades and a glass grill hold.

And then I return to myself, a photocopy of the person I will be
yesterday and the day
tomorrow, alone with my reflection in a lonely metal tube, an anti
oxidant or pathogen,
radical running late to a meeting on the loading dock for the
Central Library.

Chapter 8

Edric Mesmer

This form of poem I've come to think of as the "bibliograph," lending weight as it does to the sources of its own informing.

The poem is derived from a search for the keywords [Ann] and [Goldsmith]—the first and last names of my dear friend, poet Ann Goldsmith—in the online catalog of Lockwood Memorial Library, the search results restricted to the holdings of that library—the floors of which loom above me as I catalog. The occasion, Ann's eighty-fourth turn around the sun.

From each book retrieved from the stacks I selected a line from its eighty-fourth page. Sometimes this was itself a citation, or a graphic illustration, or included a quotation from another text. The samples were then arranged into something playing at harmony to my ear. So there is a great deal of intentionality, even as chance informs the parameters: what books have been selected for our library by the research interests of our community; the scholarly nature of the institution; the coincidence of Ann's surname and that of the frequently anthologized Oliver Goldsmith; Ann's own appearance in the anthology *Poets at Work*, the eighty-fourth page of which features a poem by her friend the late poet Jimmie Gilliam; and what books were checked out or missing at the time of this search. (In the instance of the Ann Orr catalog, the pagination did not reach "84," so I had to circle round to page 15, being the eighty-fourth after reaching the end and counting forward.)

I think, symbolically, the library's holdings represent the "word bank" of our lexicon, or the known swathe of collective knowledge each researcher illuminates a path through. Intentionally constrained for this poetic exercise, the poem reveals how we still might maneuver within such constraint.

[Ann] [Goldsmith], 84

Edric Mesmer

Stormwater runoff plays an important role in the pollution of the
Bay. Unlike[1]

longitudinal investigation. *Brain and Language, 28,* 159-168[2]

their lordships took the hint, and did not emigrate.[3]

20. Claude McKay. "Harlem Shadows," in *Harlem Shadows* (New
York, Har-[4]

mocracy [is] savage and wild." "A simple democracy…is one of
the greatest[5]

Of these historious tales[6]

other nonverbal art—visual-verbal games are serious play.[7]

To evaluate their typology, Dillard et al. (1989, Study 1) used a
strategy rejection procedure.[8]

Republic: "The temperate struggles of the patricians and plebeians[9]
became the focus of attention. The model tested by these social

---

1. Stephen Goldsmith and Donald F Kettl, *Unlocking the Power of Networks: Keys to High-Performance Government* (Cambridge, MA: Washington, D.C.: Ash Institute for Democratic Governance and Innovation, 2009), 84.

2. Nancy C. Jordan and Josephine Goldsmith-Phillips, *Learning Disabilities: New Directions for Assessment and Intervention* (Boston, MA: Allyn and Bacon, 1994), 84.

3. Samuel Eliot Morison, *Builders of the Bay Colony* Boston, MA: New York, NY: Houghton Mifflin Company, 1930, 84.

4. Catherine Rottenberg, *Black Harlem and the Jewish Lower East Side: Narratives Out of Time,* Albany, NY: State University of New York Press, 2013, 84.

5. Don E. Eberly, *Building a Healthy Culture: Strategies for an American Renaissance,* Grand Rapids, MI: W.B. Eerdmans Pub. Co., 2001, 84.

6. [John Skelton.] Margaret W. Ferguson, Mary Jo Salter, and Jon Stallworthy, eds., *The Norton Anthology of Poetry.* New York, NY: Norton, 2005, 84.

7. James L. Thomas, *Nonprint in the Elementary Curriculum: Readings for Reference,* Littleton, CO: Libraries Unlimited, 1982, 84.

8. Bryan B. Whaley and Wendy Santer, *Explaining Communication: Contemporary Theories and Exemplars,* Mahwah, NJ: Lawrence Erlbaum Associates, 2007, 84.

9. Frederick W. (Frederick Whiley) Hilles, *The Age of Johnson: Essays Presented to Chauncey Brewster Tinker,* New Haven, CT: Yale University Press, 1949, 84.

learning theorists[10]

Genius, to do more to agitate, than all the Allied Sovereigns to
tranquilize,[11]

doomed men should all. Shouts were raised; ravens circled, the
eagle[12]

vision that was available to later poets—Collins, Dyer, and
Cowper—for[13]

constraint in samples of continuous prose. Unpublished Doctoral
dissertation,[14]

Why Change a Winning Formula?[15]

This measures how the respondent perceives norms in his or her
peer group.[16]

sibling tells child to "go give Mommy a kiss and tell her you're
sorry."[17]

daddy loved mother and never the twain[18]

---

10. Charles A. (Charles Alexander) Nelson, *Threats to Optimal Development: Integrating Biological, Psychological, and Social Risk Factors*, Hillsdale, N.J.: L. Erlbaum Associates, 1994, 84.

11. [Stendhal's *Memoirs of Rossini*.] Tom Mole, *Romanticism and Celebrity Culture, 1750-1850*, Cambridge: Cambridge University Press, 2009, 84.

12. [The Battle of Maldon.] M. H. (Meyer Howard) Abrams, *The Norton Anthology of English Literature*, New York, NY: Norton, 1986, 84.

13. Dustin H. Griffin, *Patriotism and Poetry in Eighteenth-Century Britain*, Cambridge; New York: Cambridge University Press, 2002, 84.

14. National Reading Conference (U.S.) and Frank Greene *Investigations Relating to Mature Reading*, Milwaukee, WI: National Reading Conference, 1972, 84.

15. Frances Hesselbein and Paul M. Cohen, *Leader to Leader: Enduring Insights On Leadership from the Drucker Foundation's Award-winning Journal*, San Francisco, CA: Jossey-Bass, 1999, 84.

16. Peter K. Smith, *Emotional and Behavioural Difficulties Associated with Bullying and Cyberbullying*, New York, NY: London: Routledge, Taylor & Francis Group, 2014, 84.

17. Celia A. Brownell and Claire B. Kopp, *Socioemotional Development in the Toddler Years: Transitions and Transformations*, New York, NY: Guilford Press, 2007, 84.

18. [Jimmie Gilliam.] Betty Cohen, ed. *Poets at Work: Contemporary Poets—Lives, Poems, Process*, Buffalo, NY: Just Buffalo Literary Center, 1995, 84.

I dream at night of having a house of my own.[19]
public policy, feminist theory, and the political economy of gender.[20]

Table 4.1 Occurrence of female and male figurines according to material at Inca ritual sites.[88]

Female figurines					Male figurines		
Gold	Silver	Copper	Shell	Stone	Gold	Silver	Shell
High-altitude shrines							
3	12		5	1	3	2	7
Túcume, Sacsahuaman and Isla de La Plata							
2	5	1	2				2
Lake Titicaca							
1					2	2	
TOTALS							
6	17	1	7	1	5	4	9

[21]

The range of work she produced over the years is remarkable From[22]
out "all about gilding the eastern hemisphere;"[23]
Mischief on them all! I trust,' quoth he, 'the world will amend[24]
irrelevance, or that the changes required by them are merely extensions of[25]

19. Bill Bigelow and Bob Peterson, *Rethinking Globalization: Teaching for Justice in an Unjust World*, Milwaukee, WI: Rethinking Schools Press, 2002, 84.

20. James Cicarelli and Julianne Cicarelli, *Distinguished Women Economists*, Westport, CT: Greenwood Press, 2003, 84.

21. Colin McEwan, British Museum, and Museum of Mankind. *Precolumbian Gold: Technology, Style and Iconography*, Chicago: Fitzroy Dearborn Publishers, 2000, 84.

22. Lane Coulter, et al, *Ann Orr: Silversmith, Goldsmith, & Enamelist*, Athens, GA: Georgia Museum of Art, University of Georgia, 1994, 15.

23. Walter Scott, *Biographical Memoirs of Eminent Novelists, and Other Distinguished Persons*, Freeport, NY: Books for Libraries Press, 1972, Vol. 1, 84.

24. Walter Scott, *Biographical Memoirs of Eminent Novelists, and Other Distinguished Persons*, Freeport, NY: Books for Libraries Press, 1972, Vol. 2, 84.

25. Paul S. Pottinger and Joan Goldsmith, *Defining and Measuring Competence*, San Francisco: Jossey-Bass, 1979, 84.

plot as contributing to the play a tone of sexual innuendo; but[26] *differently.*[27]

Europe ridicules our system. The idea entertained on the Continent upon such occasions is silence[28]

The Author. A Poem (London: Printed for W.   *and Fragment of Journey. Volume II* (London:[29]

largely overlooking assessment of the effects stigma has on status dis-[30]

encounters: An analysis of physician and patient communication in a primary care setting.[31]

that on the ashes of his youth doth lie,[32]

by 22 to 22 by 25 inches. He did many other well-known personages in this[33]

human life. *Brideshead Revisited* is no   When Charles Ryder met Sebastian[34]

26. Stanley W. Wells, *English Drama, Excluding Shakespeare: Select Bibliographical Guides*, London; New York: Oxford University Press, 1975, 84.

27. Frances Hesselbein, Marshall Goldsmith, Iain Somerville, and Peter F. Drucker Foundation for Nonprofit Management, *Leading for Innovation and Organizing for Results*, San Francisco, CA: Jossey-Bass, 2002, 84.

28. A. Norman (Alexander Norman) Jeffares and Peter Van de Kamp, *Irish Literature: The Eighteenth Century*, Dublin: Irish Academic Press, 2006, 84.

29. John E. Sitter, *Eighteenth-Century British Poets*, vol. 109, Detroit: Gale Research, 1991, 84.

30. Timothy Edgar, Seth M Noar, and Vicki S Freimuth. *Communication Perspectives On HIV/AIDS for the 21st Century*, New York, NY: Lawrence Erlbaum Associates/Taylor & Francis Group, 2008, 84.

31. Teresa L. Thompson, *Handbook of Health Communication*, Mahwah, NJ: Lawrence Erlbaum Associates, 2003, 84.

32. [William Shakespeare.] William Harmon, *The Top 500 Poems*, New York, NY: Columbia University Press, 1992, 84.

33. Jean Lipman and Alice Winchester, *Primitive Painters in America, 1750-1950: An Anthology*, New York, NY: Dodd, Mead, 1950, 84.

34. Frank N. (Frank Northen) Magill, ed., *Masterpieces of World Literature in Digest Form*, New York, NY: Harper, 1952, 84.

"Whooey."[35]
ful. The play humorously satirizes the stereo-   had "a
    masculinity and energy found in the
                                                    work[36]
about deliberately distancing herself from him, from the court,
    and from her[37]

even within the roles that have been assigned to her, she has[38]
her state treasure of heaped nonsense:
    Prose swell'd to verse, verse loit'ring into prose:[39]
Curse on his perjured arts! dissembling smooth![40]
they take the sign, and the substance too. And by that Scripture
    which she once abus'd[41]

35. Jack Barry Ludwig and Richard Poirier, *Stories, British and American*, Boston, MA: Houghton Mifflin, 1953, 84.

36. William H. New, **Canadian Writers Before 1890**, Detroit, MI: Gale Research, 1990, Vol. 99, 84.

37. Faith Evelyn Beasley and Katharine Ann Jensen, *Approaches to Teaching Lafayette's the Princess of Clèves*, New York, NY: Modern Language Association of America, 1998, 84.

38. Willa Shalit, *Becoming Myself: Reflections On Growing Up Female*, New York, NY: Hyperion, 2006, 84.

39. [Alexander Pope.] Larry S. Champion, *Quick Springs of Sense: Studies in the Eighteenth Century*, Athens, GA: University of Georgia Press, 1974, 84.

40. [Robert Burns.] Ernest Bernbaum, *Anthology of Romanticism*, New York, NY: Ronald Press Co, 1948, 84.

41. [John Dryden.] Louis I. (Louis Ignatius) Bredvold, *Eighteenth Century Poetry & Prose*, New York, NY: Ronald Press Co, 1956, 84.

Clauses escaping from within archival asylum as breath

Edric Mesmer

had you ever to focus on furnaces? I'd
not, but an ancestor had, and
so I feel it's in my blood, if only, plied

at, beyond the barb-tongued *ad hominem* assassins;
and I—falling hard on the edifices of institutions—
taken refuge within, quarantined as by a
                    quavery etude;

I enter into the archive as would-
be panopticon, absented of center,
pineal thought stemmed between:

where two spines might lie, side-by-side, upon the
shelf-coffin, hidden in leather, or within the clutch
of a broad or diminutive hand,
                    phoenixing

shhhhhhhhhhhhhhhhhhhhhhhhhhhhh!
a poem is opening within the poem…:
                    E: where does poetry come from?
                    N: where does music come from?

is it no longer vogue to name names
within the poem? (but who will mend
the moon?) (who, the
                    bathing costumes?)

caryatids pace atop pentagonals,
atria communicating collections like spleens—these collections!
O, the collections we have

cataloged in song...
edges of a thought yet unworn...
a common chisel could
                    do no more.

Chapter 9

SORTING NOISES: POETRY, LIBRARIES, AND THE RESISTANCE OF INFORMATION

Sam Lohmann

"Appearance of the world, disappearance of coherence"
—Lyn Hejinian, *The Unfollowing*

Librarians and poets are fatuous experts on everything. Both have had frequent recourse to information theories ranging from cybernetics to semiotics and from corporate parsimonies to hermetic correspondences. I wanted to start a movement, LIBRARIANS AGAINST INFORMATION, in solidarity with POETS AGAINST LITERATURE. Instead, I wrote this essay, borrowing a dilapidated conceit: Russell Ackoff's so-called Wisdom Pyramid. Picture a triangle, laterally stratified, hierarchic and vaguely hieratic: from bottom to top, the steps are Data, Information, Knowledge, and Wisdom.[1] Imagine this as poetry. I tried, playing sorts with whatever came to hand, heaping questions, tweaking answers and scattering rubble.

---

1. Russell Ackoff, "From Data to Wisdom," *Journal of Applied Systems Analysis* 16 (1989): 3-9. As many have noted, the scheme was anticipated in T.S. Eliot's *Four Quartets* and elsewhere. For a review of permutations, see Jennifer Rowley, "The wisdom hierarchy: representations of the DIKW hierarchy," *Journal of Information Science* 33, no. 2 (2007): 163-180.

DATA/POLLEN/NOISE

Look 'em up: Contingent, material, sensible (if unsensed), countable (if countless), transfers of earthly earth never worldly, data are for example before example, overample, peaks and valleys of a first fricative in its groundless granularity. Data are both irreducible particles and indigestible enormities: like, information's atoms, or information before differentiation, dissolute but reactive: bumps but not phrenology, illegible bumps, maybe words before we read them, maybe our infinite to-read lists, maybe lemures, wergild, and pleroma. Up-to-date librarians have fallen into data with characteristic obsequiousness, dragging along traditions of metadata classification which were always already knowledge obverted into facile authoritarian wisdom.

Poets, with characteristic stubbornness and lazy stride, have always inhabited a world of data—but I must mean two incompatible kinds of data. Data resist the intelligence almost successfully. Poets should resist success almost intelligently. Librarians should use data to hold knowledge at bay. At bay is in clover, we love data, and data anyway *are* inevitable and not the problem. Data—singular, a sort of swarm, sometimes big, sometimes raw, prey to lots of misleading cognitive and neural analogies—*is* the problem for librarians. And for poets—everything can compose, but nobody can keep up with the grand composition.

Data seems to answer our voraciousness, becoming singular the more plural we try to get. We can't help scanning it for messages or a message: *Don't think, look; or Don't look now.* And by the time you're doing anything with data it's already something else. Data is an abstraction of abstractions, metametaphor posing as ultimate concreteness. Before data, the reigning metaphor was *pollen,*[2]

---

2. Pollen is another singular noun that should really be plural—unless it's the Greek *pollen aporian,* which I need to look up. (I did. As I vaguely recalled, it means a problem without a solution. Google Books informs me that Aristotle used this phrase in reference to both the reproduction of honeybees and the location of phantasmal images within the soul.)

favored by Novalis who gathered stray *Pollen and Fragments*, and by Aimé Césaire who invented the most astonishing metadata field:

Desert, desert, I endure your challenge
blank to be filled out on the passport of pollen.[3]

If not pollen on the desert winds, it's *noise* we talk about. Not noises—winds, sands—since this metaphor works to push aside, for now, all questions of differentiation or message, as in Gregory Bateson's truism: "All that is not information, not redundancy, not form and not restraints—is noise, the only possible source of *new* patterns."[4] Aggregate noise rushed in when we needed it (hegemonic *we*), mid-20th century when telecommunications metastasized into computing. But to a different we, we who love noise, the figure—the ground—is still vivid. What's unanticipated and unpatterned gives place and impulse to patterning.

Can you decompose language into noise? James Yeary took an allegorically literal approach in a prose work, "Mops," a list of 563 one-word sentences he's described as "imaginary verbs": "Buckets. Choke. Vino. Squirrels. Reality. Tumescence. Brickwork. Drone. Succotash. Exhaust. Ceramics. Eye. Mario. Soup. Wax. Scams. Glow. Perseverance. Duck."[5] Which isn't noise, though Yeary has meticulously obstructed any clear paths for meaning or overt patterns of sound, varying syllable counts and avoiding alliteration between adjacent words, so that the exception "Wax. Scams." jumps out while the three *ucks* remain inconspicuous because dispersed. Noise is an imaginative category with potential to verb.

---

3. Aimé Césaire, *The Collected Poetry*, translated by Clayton Eshleman and Annette Smith (Berkeley: University of California, 1983), 354 (my translation).

4. Gregory Bateson, "Cybernetic Explanation," in *Steps to an Ecology of Mind* (New York: Ballantine, 1972), 410. Redundancy is cybernetics jargon for whatever is part of some recognizable pattern and therefore "restrains" or limits the possibilities elsewhere in the same system.

5. James Yeary, "Mops," in *Rolling in the Easy Circumstances* by James Yeary and Sam Lohmann (n.p.: Great Fainting Spells, 2012), [6].

INFORMATION, OR BERRYPICKING

"Mops" is a poem in that it invites play. Helplessly, of course, you start playing or informing as soon as two words appear. Attempts to reverse-engineer language into raw noise backfire yielding imaginary verbs, germinating pollen. The Wisdom Pyramid's nonsense, but the jump from nonsense into redundancy, bewilderment into composition, matters if poetry and libraries are sites for living, rather than naively instrumental conduits of *information* (or *expression*). Don't understand but experience, use information. From library discourse I'm tempted to borrow the term "sense-making," emphasizing (I wish librarians would) an active making in all senses (all twenty-seven, beloved Anna Blume!).

My favorite sense-making right now is this Art Ensemble of Chicago record, *Full Force*, a hand-me-down from my mother-in-law. I listen over and over. The whole thing's a complex, heterogeneous concord, full of gradual or sudden moments of sense, making separate lines gather and correspond into a given shape from diverging tunes. Ending Side 1, the lumpy sprawl of the first track, "Magg Zelma," full of ghostly cackles and counterspiraling noisy layers, suddenly clenches into the 45-second fanfare "Care Free," which seems to transpose and compress the whole foregoing meander into a single (however duplicitous, wayward and gappy) declarative melody.

The 1980 album seems to study the transition two decades earlier from late bebop to free jazz—as if an evolution could be replayed synchronically. By 1980 the polemical experiment of free collective improvisation no longer had to push against entrenched traditions—it *was* tradition—and could be understood as cognitive, aesthetic experience, conversation emerging as an ensemble of noisers gathers up its possible musics, ear against ear and moment to moment: like Bach's "reasonable men in an orderly discussion," with parameters of order and ratio thrown far afield: the best evidence I've found lately of human intelligences acting collectively.

Another sense-making: Whit Griffin's poetry of information, which quilts together shreds of lapsed wisdom from countless sources, conjuring a choral arcane out of dusty, lively libraries. Each shred's a marvel in itself, but it's the stitches that fascinate:

> The starling's
> bill turns from black to yellow. The Athenians wore golden
> grasshoppers in their hair. Hearn tells us the Dorians wrote
> on toadstools. The shaggy-cap melts drop by drop. The grouse
> grows appendages on its toes to aid walking in winter. As the
> halcyon nests about the time of the winter solstice. The Sphinx
> was the daughter of Echidna and Typhon.[6]

The reader, entering anywhere, gets pulled both forwards and back by a relational prosody. Maybe this is what library literature calls a "visceral information need" or, in Marcia Bates's metaphor, information-seeking as berrypicking.[7] Berry to berry or starling to Typhon we've drifted far from the simplistic signal/noise model, foundational for information and library discourses since it was proposed—in military and corporate telecommunications contexts—by Claude Shannon in the 1940s. But the action of "redundancy" still matters—filtering, sorting, transforming. I still like the pragmatic openness of Bateson's non-definition: any "difference which makes a difference," within a given system, *informs*.[8]

BEWILDERMENT, OR USEFUL KNOWLEDGE

Knowledge is data's delirium, where the pyramid begins to mushroom. Just as data and information, on the signal/noise

---

6. Whit Griffin, *We Who Saw Everything* (Brooklyn, NY: The Cultural Society, 2015), 93.

7. Robert S. Taylor, "Question Negotiation and Information Seeking in Libraries," *College and Research Libraries* 29, no. 3 (1968): 178-194; Marcia Bates, "The Design of Browsing and Berrypicking Techniques for the Online Search Onterface," *Online Review* 13, no. 5 (1989): 407-424, retrieved from https://pages.gseis.ucla.edu/faculty/bates/berrypicking.html.

8. Bateson, "Form, Substance and Difference," in *Steps to an Ecology of Mind*, 453.

model, became paradigmatic in the postwar military-industrial information rush, the next tier was canonized in the 1980s: knowledge conceived as mechanical economy, as in knowledge creation, knowledge management, knowledge banking. The Wisdom Pyramid, popularized at this point, essentially adds a layer or two of neoliberal management-mysticism to the information discourse.[9] At our most pompous and self-regarding, librarians have seen ourselves as guardians of knowledge. Poets characteristically claim to guard something even more totalizing: language itself—whether as termites, clownfish, or unlegislated acknowledgers.

But there's Césaire's magnificent essay "Poetry and Knowledge."[10] And Robin Blaser's vocation to uncover knowledge loosed from predatory positivisms.[11] For Césaire, poetry's knowledge embodies the "individual whole"—a situated microcosm, participating among others in what must be a magic ecology, imaginal, like Blaser's Image-Nations or José Lezama Lima's imaginary eras. Césaire writes:

> What presides over the poem is not the most lucid intelligence, or the most acute sensibility, but an entire experience . . . the most extraordinary contacts: all the pasts, all the futures (the anticyclone builds its plateau, the amoeba loses its pseudopods, vanished vegetations meet). All the flux, all the rays.[12]

I don't have these poets' polymath brilliance and prefer to claim not knowledge through poetry but bewilderment in poetry,

---

9. For a historical summary and an interesting commentary on Ackoff, see David Weinberger, *Too Big to Know: Rethinking Knowledge Now That the Facts aren't Facts, Experts are Everywhere, and the Smartest Person in the Room is the Room* (New York: Basic Books, 2011), 1-5.

10. Translated by A. James Arnold, in *Césaire's Lyric and Dramatic Poetry 1946-82*, trans. Clayton Eshleman and Annette Smith (Charlottesville: University of Virginia, 1990), xlii-lvi.

11. See especially Blaser's essay "Poetry and Positivisms: High Muck-a-Muck or 'Spiritual Ketchup'" in *The Fire: Collected Essays of Robin Blaser*, ed. Miriam Nichols (Berkeley: University of California, 2006), 38-63; and the section titled "Moderns and Contemporaries: The Knowledge of the Poet" in *The Astonishment Tapes: Talks on Poetry and Autobiography with Robin Blaser and Friends*, ed. Nichols (Tuscaloosa, AL: University of Alabama, 2015), 164-226.

12. Césaire, "Poetry and Knowledge," xlvii-xlviii.

following Fanny Howe.[13] If knowledge is information put to work by understanding, bewilderment is where understanding struggles, among irreconcilable informations and wild data, to dwell and participate in the out-of-phase goosegabble village, the real. If bewilderment is a form of wisdom, wisdom isn't the facility Ackoff proposed. Bewilderment's wisdom is hazardous and forlorn like trying to write poems in a library—but why be grandiose? It's only the commotion of composition— Gertrude Stein's "human mind" activity, distinct from "human nature."

Words convey meanings, but only within a constrained universe of differences that make differences—whether cosmic or particulate. Stein foresees "Mops":

> I found that any kind of a book if you read with glasses on and somebody is cutting your hair and so you cannot keep your glasses on and you use your glasses as a magnifying glass and so read word by word reading word by word makes the writing that is not anything be something.
>
> Very regrettable but very true.[14]

In composition—as opposed to communication—each word bewilders by bringing many kinds of information to a focus.

Not only the semantic and symbolic meanings, but all the sonic and graphic qualities of words start to nudge and taste each other. Prosody is present to them all. Among poets this is vapid shop talk, but could it usefully divert or block the library information-to-knowledge conduit? What would happen if, instead of Ackoff's abstracted and at best "actionable" currency, library workers had Césaire's cosmological, processual knowledge in mind? Flare-ups of bewilderment? Or an ecology of attention? I like to imagine a personism of librarianship after Frank O'Hara, with bewilderment,

---

13. See the essay "Bewilderment" in Howe's book *The Wedding Dress: Meditations on Word and Life* (Berkeley: University of California, 2003), 5-23.

14. Gertrude Stein, *A Geographical History of America or the Relation of Human Nature to the Human Mind* (New York: Random House, 1936), 115.

knowledge or words Lucky-Pierre-style between two people not two pages.[15]

LIBRARY AS DRAGON

But I may have broken the context. Stein's next sentence rejects any nostalgia for wholes: "So that shows to you that the whole thing is not interesting because as a whole well as a whole there has to be remembering and forgetting, but one at a time, oh one at a time is something oh yes definitely something." Stein's human mind never remembers: "it knows and it writes what it knows."[16] Spontaneous knowledge! What about meaning without redundancy, that is without pattern and without memory—is that just noise, an excessive openness or even attachment to what isn't a signal?

Bateson, adapting Shannon, reduced information to redundancies: mutually delimiting possibilities within a given "universe." Donald Case, distorting Bateson's context, stipulates that information's differences should make differences to "a conscious, human mind."[17] Does that help? Alluringly, cybernetics renders everything schematic, but *everything*, without precluding the information present in tone, texture and tune (you just gotta ask the right universe). Again there's a jump or pop between levels, figured by H.D.'s painter "who concentrated on one tuft of pine branch with its brown cone until every needle bore to every other one, a clear relationship like a drawing of a later mechanical twentieth century bridge builder."[18]

Or by Lezama: "The fascinations of those archetypal groupings, of the magnetizing that convokes in order to flee from the whirl

---

15. Frank O'Hara, "Personism: A Manifesto," in *The Collected Poems of Frank O'Hara*, ed. Donald Allen (New York: Knopf, 1971), 498-499.

16. Stein, *A Geographical History of America*, 115 and 111.

17. Donald O. Case, *Looking for Information: A Survey of Research on Information Seeking, Needs, and Behavior* (London: Academic Press, 2002), 40.

18. H.D., *Notes on Thought and Vision* (San Francisco: City Lights, 1982), 42-43.

that must be reduced to the law of its structure."[19] Lezama, with his enigmas of image, is moving to the center. His essay "Confluences" investigates what he calls *supernature*, quoting Pascal: "Since true nature has been lost, everything can be nature." Lezama contrasts the "determinism of nature" with "the total freedom of the image" figured in a childhood memory of "that room, library, storeroom, resting place for wayward things," where he perceived "all the sparks of an unseen forge."

Which develops into the *library as dragon*, the "defensive labyrinth" of poetry's resistance:

> There, in solitude, one seeks company, and more specifically in public libraries, where company seeks solitude. The struggle against the dragon had to take place in the ceaseless relationships between solitude and company . . . And just as it is claimed in some medieval legend that the devil likes to sleep in the shadow of a bell tower, so the uncreated that creates likes to spend the day in the library, because the library has begun by being something unheard, unseen, and thus nature will be found in supernature. [20]

I find this eerily comforting if not quite comprehensible. I'd place it beside the opening to Lisa Robertson's essay on noise: "I wanted the present to be an ideal library. Infinity, plenum, chaos, dust. I wanted it to be an agora—total availability of the entire thick history of linguistic conviviality and the ability to be completely lost in the strangeness of civic description." Robertson suggests the library is a city and defines city as "a peopled-through sensing."[21] So in place of "wisdom" comes the image of the library—peopled-through, disquiet, indiscriminate, bedragoned—that abdicates its authority to let polyphony in.

19. José Lezama Lima, "Procession," trans. James Irby, in *Jose Lezama Lima: Selections*, ed. Ernesto Livon-Grossman (Berkeley: University of California, 2005).

20. Lezama Lima, "Confluences," trans. Irby, in *Selections*, 104 and 114-116.

21. Lisa Robertson, "Disquiet," in *Nilling: Prose Essays on Noise, Pornography, the Codex, Melancholy, Lucretius, Folds, Cities and Related Aporias* (Toronto: Bookthug, 2012), 57.

UNFOLLOWING UNUNDERSTANDING, OR
SCRATCHES ON THE RECORD

Poetry might teach librarians to see information as not only social, but sociable. In associating, it also resists, doubling, disobeying—*unfollowing*, to use Lyn Hejinian's recent coinage, the title of a work built painstakingly of non-sequiturs. Some reject the noisy excess of non-sequitur as a loss of focus, as in Mary Butts' characterization: "Voluble and mobile, Ambrose had a trick of statement, one to each sentence, followed by a denial, a reversal of it in the next. So that which seemed, sentence by sentence, to be a vivid reaction to life, cancelled out to nothing. To no belief at all."[22]

But Hejinian pursues the unfollowing precisely as a vivid reaction to death. Hilarity and uncertainty, she makes clear, are indices of loss.

> Laughter is encrypted grief, but grief is encrypted laughter, too
> …
> The sun burns every story to a crisp and leaves only a lisp, or lapse,
> palsy, panic or a princess pointing at something across another
> now
> …
> The sociable book is ample and uninhibited, unashamed of its jolly
> idiosyncracies, unembarrassed by its infuriated sentimentality
> — o lucky sociable book off the shelf
> …
> Survival can't wait[23]

In place of a monument or wisdom as such. Noise, resistance, mourning, static, pollen, dust.

Noise as record. Reference as resistance. Robertson: "Noise exceeds its own identity. It is the extreme of difference. Noise is the non-knowledge of meaning, the by-product of economies."[24]

---

22. Mary Butts, "Green," in *From Altar to Chimney-Piece: Selected Stories* (Kingston, NY: McPherson & Co., 1992), 65.

23. Lyn Hejinian, *The Unfollowing* (Richmond, CA: Omnidawn, 2016), 81.

24. Robertson, "Disquiet," 57.

Nathaniel Mackey: ". . . I accept it all, even the scratches and the nicks, the points on the record where the needle skips. Noisy reminders of the wear of time they may well be, but I hear them as rickety, quixotic rungs on a discontinuous ladder . . ."[25] The omnivorous poet, *amateur de toutes les choses* (Lezama, quoting La Fontaine) or "scientist of the whole" (Robert Kelly),[26] basketweaving or berrypicking, eats noise, churns dust like butter.

Can we love archives while rejecting institutional triumphalism? I deliberate about librarianship as a deliberation with ghosts, guarding not knowledge but tangles of gaps, animadversions, unbeliefs, forked tongues and invisible sparks. Can we imagine information unpatterned, or ask, with Morton Feldman, *Why Patterns?* Listening to Feldman's trio I can only find it demandingly patterned; irregular, but no more so than Stanley Whitney's grids or the hand-woven kilim Feldman loved to stare at. Robertson again: "The rhythmic opacity of noise or the body or the city fails or exceeds its measure. Listening leans expectantly towards a pattern that is effacing itself . . . "[27]

"Understanding" is sometimes wedged between knowledge and wisdom, so now I want blasphemously to bring in Jack Spicer's word *ununderstanding* from "A Textbook of Poetry": another one-word sentence, another imaginary verb: "A private language. Carried about us, them. Ununderstanding."[28] But surely ununderstanding, like language, takes two, and is no more private than the *sense-making* (Brenda Dervin) or *formulation* (Carroll C.

---

25. Nathaniel Mackey, Djbot Baghostus's Run (Los Angeles: Sun and Moon, 1993), as quoted in the essay "Blue in Green: Black Interiority" in Mackey's *Paracritical Hinge: Essays, Talks, Notes, Interviews* (Madison: University of Wisconsin, 2004), 206.

26. Armando Alvarez Bravo, "An Interview with José Lezama Lima," trans. Irby, in *Selections*, 126; Robert Kelly, "Re: Snow Jobs / we have got:", in *A Voice Full of Cities: The Collected Essays of Robert Kelly*, ed. Pierre Joris and Peter Cockelbergh (New York: Contra Mundum, 2014), 103.

27. Robertson, "Disquiet," 61.

28. Jack Spicer, "A Textbook of Poetry," in *My Vocabulary Did This to Me: The Collected Poetry of Jack Spicer*, ed. Peter Gizzi and Kevin Killian (Middletown, CT: Wesleyan University Press, 2010), 313.

Kuhlthau)[29] that teaching librarians make a holy grail of. Much less has been made of Bateson's astonishing definition of wisdom: "a sense or recognition of the fact of circuitry" needed, in an ecology of "circuit structures," for love to survive.[30]

Bibliography

Ackoff, Russell. "From Data to Wisdom." *Journal of Applied Systems Analysis* 16 (1989): 3-9.

Art Ensemble of Chicago. *Full Force*. ECM 1779873, 1980, LP.

Bates, Marcia. "The Design of Browsing and Berrypicking Techniques for the Online Search Interface." *Online Review* 13, no. 5 (1989): 407-424. https://pages.gseis.ucla. edu/faculty/bates/berrypicking.html.

Bateson, Gregory. *Steps to an Ecology of Mind*. New York: Ballantine, 1972.

Blaser, Robin. *The Fire: Collected Essays of Robin Blaser*. Edited by Miriam Nichols. Berkeley: University of California, 2006.

———. *The Astonishment Tapes: Talks on Poetry and Autobiography with Robin Blaser and Friends*. Edited by Miriam Nichols. Tuscaloosa, AL: University of Alabama, 2015.

Butts, Mary. *From Altar to Chimney-Piece: Selected Stories*. Kingston, NY: McPherson & Co. 1992.

---

29. Brenda Dervin, "An Overview of Sense-Making Research: Concepts, Methods and Results," paper presented at the annual meeting of the International Communication Association, Dallas, 1983, retrieved from http://faculty. washington.edu/wpratt/MEBI598/Methods/An%20Overview%20of%20 Sense-Making%20Research%201983a.htm; Carroll Collier Kuhlthau, *Seeking Meaning: A Process Approach to Library and Information Services*, 2nd ed. (Westport, CT: Libraries Unlimited, 2004).

30. Bateson, "Style, Grace and Information in Primitive Art," in *Steps to an Ecology of Mind*, 146.

Case, Donald O. *Looking for Information: A Survey of Research on Information Seeking, Needs, and Behavior.* London: Academic Press, 2002.

Césaire, Aimé. *The Collected Poetry.* Translated by Clayton Eshleman and Annette Smith. Berkeley: University of California, 1983.

———. *Lyric and Dramatic Poetry 1946-82.* Translated by Clayton Eshleman and Annette Smith. Charlottesville: University of Virginia, 1990.

H. D. *Notes on Thought and Vision.* San Francisco: City Lights, 1982.

Dervin, Brenda. "An Overview of Sense-Making Research: Concepts, Methods and Results." Paper presented at the annual meeting of the International Communication Association, Dallas, TX, 1983. http://faculty.washington. edu/wpratt/MEBI598/Methods/An%20Overview%20 of%20Sense-Making%20Research%201983a.htm

Feldman, Morton. *Rothko Chapel/Why Patterns?* California E.A.R. Unit. New Albion Records, 1991, compact disc.

Griffin, Whit. *We Who Saw Everything.* Brooklyn, NY: The Cultural Society, 2015.

Hejinian, Lyn. *The Unfollowing.* Richmond, CA: Omnidawn, 2016.

Howe, Fanny. *The Wedding Dress: Meditations on Word and Life.* Berkeley: University of California, 2003.

Kelly, Robert. *A Voice Full of Cities: The Collected Essays of Robert Kelly.* Edited by Pierre Joris and Peter Cockelbergh. New York: Contra Mundum, 2014.

Kuhlthau, Carroll Collier. *Seeking Meaning: A Process Approach to Library and Information Services.* 2nd edition. Westport, CT: Libraries Unlimited, 2004.

Lezama Lima, José. *José Lezama Lima: Selections*. Edited by
Ernesto Livon-Grossman. Berkeley: University of
California, 2005.

Mackey, Nathaniel. *Paracritical Hinge: Essays, Talks, Notes, Interviews*.
Madison: University of Wisconsin, 2004.

Robertson, Lisa. *Nilling: Prose Essays on Noise, Pornography, the Codex,
Melancholy, Lucretius, Folds, Cities, and Related Aporias*.
Toronto: Bookthug, 2012.

Rowley, Jennifer. "The Wisdom Hierarchy: Representations of the
DIKW Hierarchy." *Journal of Information Science* 33, no. 2
(2007): 163-180. doi: 10.1177/0165551506070706.

Spicer, Jack. *My Vocabulary Did This to Me: The Collected Poetry of
Jack Spicer*. Edited by Peter Gizzi and Kevin Killian.
Middletown, CT: Wesleyan University, 2010.

Stein, Gertrude. *A Geographical History of America or the Relation of
Human Nature to the Human Mind*. New York: Random
House, 1936.

Taylor, Robert S. "Question Negotiation and Information Seeking
in Libraries." *College and Research Libraries* 29, no. 3
(1968): 178-194.

Weinberger, David. *Too Big to Know: Rethinking Knowledge Now
That the Facts aren't Facts, Experts are Everywhere, and the
Smartest Person in the Room is the Room*. New York: Basic
Books, 2011.

Yeary, James, and Sam Lohmann. *Rolling in the Easy Circumstances*.
N.p.: Great Fainting Spells, 2012.

In the Cards

Sam Lohmann

From the palms comes a sandy sound
From the tongue come many predicaments
From legend comes menswear
From the oak leaf comes a minor genre of drawing
Reliefs emerge from the dark
From cheating come ballads
From a kiss comes Isn't it funny or It isn't funny
Clocks come from sundials
From biting comes gratuitous explication
Which rises out of the ground
Popcorn comes in a bucket
From delight comes urgent lucid sharp rehearsal
From a trapdoor you get character

From ballads come legends
But red comes from menswear
From gratuitous explication you get trapdoors
From character comes losing
Which causes a ripple
From relief to shuffling
From many predicaments there appears this opening
From a minor genre of drawing comes the burn
From rehearsal, famously, comes cheating
But kissing comes from clocks
From popcorn you might get a fortune or
A sundial from It isn't funny to Isn't it funny
From a sandy sound however comes that sharp, urgent, lucid
pressing down

Chapter 10

NOTE TO SELF

Marie Elia

How can we exploit the flexibility of the narrative nature of archival description—freedom to add notes, to explain—to create documentation that invites people in? The biographical note is often the opportunity to stretch the language of description. In "RadTech Meets RadArch: Towards A New Principle for Archives and Archival Description," Jarrett M. Drake writes that "In [the biographical note], archivists often write massive memorials and monuments to wealthy, white, cisgendered and heterosexual men, including selective details about the creator that have minimal bearing on the records, and instead serve to valorize and venerate white western masculinity."[1] In libraries often named for and funded by private wealthy citizens, it is perhaps unwise, if not forbidden, to write anything other than aggrandizing biographical notes about, for example, canonical writers.

The explosion of the literary manuscript marketplace has made it challenging for academic libraries to acquire material; because of this, and because of our mission to collect widely

---

1. Jarrett M. Drake, "RadTech Meets RadArch: Towards A New Principle for Archives and Archival Description," *Medium*, April 6, 2016, accessed April 8, 2016, https://medium.com/on-archivy/radtech-meets-radarch-towards-a-new-principle-for-archives-and-archival-description-568f133e4325.

and without prejudice, we focus less on adding to our William Carlos Williams collection and more on collecting material that embodies a broader representation of 20th- and 21st-century poetry in English. Therefore, I spend most of my time processing the collections of poets who may be marginalized based on their place outside of the world of canonical poetry. Sometimes they also occupy a peripheral space based on their class or gender, but for the most part the creators whose collections I process are white men, and while poets and librarians will disagree as to whether writers' personal lives should have any bearing on their literary reception, the processing archivist is often intimately acquainted with details such as who was cheating on their spouse, who was not supporting their children, who was not paying their rent. While it is inappropriate (and unnecessary) to allow these details to color a biographical note, when I have the opportunity to do the opposite—to help contextualize or clarify biographical details when their absence portrays an image very different to an arguably more positive reality—I take extra time with my documentation and research.

According to Describing Archives: A Content Standard (DACS), the purpose of the biographical or historical note is "to describe the required elements of a biographical or administrative history note about creators embedded in the description of materials . . . This element also describes the relationship of creators to archival materials by providing information about the context in which those materials were created." Further guidelines include the following:

At the beginning of the biographical history, provide a brief summary of the most relevant aspects of a person's or family's life. Include name, dates, profession, and geographic location. (2.7.12)

Record information about the principal occupation(s) and career or lifework of persons or about the activities of families. Also indicate any other activities important to an understanding of the life of the person or family. Give information about significant accomplishments or achievements, including honors, decorations, and noteworthy public recognition. (2.7.18)

Strict adherence to this structure can make for a dry and opaque representation of a person, but for someone who is well-known or well-documented in other sources, it is enough. One consideration for archivists is that their biographical and historical notes may be the only published and public record about an obscure figure. Writing a biographical note for a collection on Charles Bukowski is as simple as relaying information that is already published and referring the user to resources for further study. (During my time as a project cataloger at the Andy Warhol Museum Archives, all of our finding aids' biographical notes consisted of a brief line referring the reader to official biographies.) However, recently I processed a collection from Panna Grady, referred to in published accounts as a socialite, girlfriend, hostess, bankroller. Her collection consists primarily of correspondence from the poets whom she supported, financially and emotionally, over the course of her lifetime, but primarily in the 1960s. She is famous for throwing parties in her Dakota apartment and giving away her money to anyone who asked. She financed magazines, plays, book tours, and living expenses, and the letters are a testament to both the appreciation and the cavalier attitudes the writers felt toward her. Some poets are grateful and sheepish at asking for more; some demand money and make clear their unequivocal expectation that it be given; and some letters—quite a few—are from wives and girlfriends of male poets, expressing gratitude and dropping little updates about the children, their home lives, their love lives.

Panna Grady shows up in a few biographies, mainly of William Burroughs, with whom she maintained a friendship and correspondence, and Philip O'Connor, her partner of nearly 30 years, but she is rarely interviewed or quoted directly. O'Connor's Wikipedia entry makes only the briefest reference to her, despite their decades-long partnership and two children. I conducted a phone interview with Panna that lasted an hour and a half, resulting in a mosaic of Post-It notes covering my desk, connected by arrows, trying to assemble a definitive biographical note for her. She is often depicted as a wealthy party girl, the black sheep who took her inheritance and ran, sleeping her way through the poetry scene. On the phone she was funny and charming and took no offense to that portrayal, but she saw herself more as a patron of the arts—albeit the kind of art where there is never any financial payoff. Patrons of painters may find themselves with artwork that appreciates, whereas patrons of Beat poetry are left holding boxes of moldering paper. Over the course of the interview she expressed constant concern over maintaining the privacy of the writers and artists she knew. In the most intimate matters, she asked that her comments be kept out of the public notes, not wanting to betray confidences. Her reticence has allowed biographers of the poets she has known to extrapolate, speculate, and most likely do their best with minimal information.

Critical librarianship as applied to archives questions the language and structure of our records—the hierarchical parent-child relationships in a finding aid, the culturally biased subject headings, the un(der)paid labor that supports research and institutions that consistently undervalue our work. Often when we talk about justice in the archives, we focus on labor, who creates the archive, who sustains it, the language that is used to discuss groups of people. A less obvious approach is to challenge yourself to think critically about the tone of a biographical note, to give it its appropriate weight and consideration. Most biographical notes and scope and content notes are written at the end of processing, an exhaustive and exhausting process that often leaves the processing archivist—or technician, or intern—a bit tired of the collection. (The joke: Never start a biographical note on a Friday afternoon.) It is generally easy enough to approach the note as one more task to check off, to write with a formulaic structure of stitched together references. It is more difficult to bear in mind that your note may be the only published official source on a person's life—that the way you frame the details will color a researcher's approach to the materials you have just spent the last week, month, year describing.

Many archivists describe their role as a supporting one, guiding the materials they describe into an identifiable organizational structure, preserving provenance and original order, and providing an order if none is recognizable. We balance what may seem to be a passive role with a regard for the voice of the collection's creator. I see the archivist's arrangement and description as closer to the work of a conservator: We respect the original and stabilize it to ensure its longevity and availability for the future. Archivists also speak of approaching their work with an objective stance. But objectivity is not neutrality: As many writers on information ethics have noted, neutrality does not exist in libraries, and every person working in them brings personal bias to the work. An archivist makes so many choices in terms of language, access points, and arrangement that necessarily prioritize some aspects of a collection over others. It is simple to use a template for a finding aid and fill it in, to highlight what we think people will look for, without trying to imagine that they might be looking for something else. Like most freedoms, the narrative structure of an archival finding aid requires accountability. The most compelling inclination for archivists is to document—not just the materials but decisions, sources of information, processes. The archivist will not just describe a collection but also tell you why she described it that way. A good archivist reveals her biases—not always explicitly, but by making her process transparent.

Unfortunately, bias can often go unchecked by the rotating cast of underfunded staff. In "Implications of Archival Labor," S. Williams writes about the un(der)paid workers in the archive, and how "people without job protections or benefits are unlikely to discuss anything about the work that is problematic."[2] A project archivist who is contracted for a year, or even two (and often just six months) is unlikely to shake things up but will likely be expected to adopt the house style of "culturally biased metadata."[3]

---

2. S. Williams, "Implications of Archival Labor," *Medium*, April 11, 2016, accessed April 12, 2016. https://medium.com/on-archivy/implications-of-archival-labor-b606d8d02014.

3. Ibid.

Even full-time archives staff members are often given job titles of "technician," never mind a faculty librarian position, which ranks them too low within the institutional hierarchy to have any effect on the system their work supports. I never intended to work in any field that was poetry-adjacent, preferring to keep the work of poetry separate from my day job. But while the field can vary widely, librarianship always requires active learning, and serving as a librarian in a poetry collection is a rare opportunity to engage constantly with poetry without the pressure of writing it or critiquing it for a living. I also never planned on being an archivist; I trained as a rare books and cataloging librarian, but my first job was as a project archivist. I realized why so many history majors turn to archives as a career: You get to be an active participant, and you get to do a lot of writing.

As a poet, I am obsessed with language, with choosing the right words in the right combination, with what is included and what is left out, and with what will be lost and what will endure. Any poet has to have enough of an ego to believe that her poems are worth writing and being read, and any archivist has to have enough sense of accountability to realize that her documentation may become the only permanent record of a person's life. If you have authority over your own work, there is a way to create a more inclusive space in a traditional archival repository. I consider writing in archives to be a core tool of our commitment to ethics within the profession. The way we write about our collections can be a way of making room for other voices within the traditional structure of archives.

Authority and authorship often part ways in the creation of finding aids, in that the authors may not have final say—in the end, authority is not always granted to the workers processing the collections. In conducting a phone interview with Panna, in carefully citing information from published sources as well as our interview, and in publishing enough personal details to contextualize the collection as well as portray her as a human being rather than an archetype, while respecting her privacy and steering clear of gossipy particulars, I hope I was able to serve the collection and the creator as well as the researcher. I am fortunate to work for an institution and within a department that values our work enough to create a full-time professional archivist position where none had existed, as well allow me to spend a morning on a phone call to the south of France to speak with Panna. Archival representation offers a unique opportunity, a little bellwether even within the term, for us to use language to represent more truths. Whereas subject analysis presents a cataloging librarian with the challenge of choosing a preexisting term to represent a work, notes fields are free-text and can be as broad or specific, predictable or provocative, as the writer feels is warranted—and can get away with. Finding aids do include subject headings for indexing, but the substance of the document for a researcher is the less obvious, the unindexable. The archivist does not editorialize in the finding aid, but instead documents decisions and sources, and offers up her bias as one more tool to navigate a collection. Every time we write a note, we are qualifying, reaching out, revealing the imperfect record and asking the user to play as active a part in reading as we have in writing.

Bibliography

Drake, Jarrett M. "RadTech Meets RadArch: Towards a New Principle for Archives and Archival Description." *Medium*, April 6, 2016. Accessed April 8, 2016. https://medium.com/on-archivy/radtech-meets-radarch-towards-a-new-principle-for-archives-and-archival-description-568f133e4325.

William, S. "Implications of Archival Labor." *Medium*, April 11, 2016. Accessed April 12, 2016. https://medium.com/on-archivy/implications-of-archival-labor-b606d8d02014.

Sources

Maria Elia

Thunder, moths, doors—we choose, as appropriate
from the following

If the set of parts is unnumbered
Then try to recognize us beyond our bodies
If the parts are sequentially numbered
Then cut your hair to get closer to the inside
If the numbering does not establish order
Then recall the Easter statuary, draped with purple veils
If there is no source that identifies the whole
Then assemble all evidence in the frame in such a way that
    we'll all wish we'd been there
But if none of the above
Then arrange your fears in order

I always thought the moths would come first
Call it guilt, call it burden of proof
from which we were instructed to choose
the appropriate source of information
the mode of issuance—our kind will stay

Chapter 11

AND LO! YR LETTER HIT ME HARD: LIVE(S) &
WORK(S) IN SPECIAL COLLECTIONS & ARCHIVES

Patrick Williams

> O sovereign was my touch
> upon the tan-ink's fragile page!
>
> Quickly, my eyes moved quickly,
> sought for smell for dust for lace
> for dry hair!
>
> -Gregory Corso
> "I Held a Shelley Manuscript (written in Houghton Library,
> Harvard)"

Just above my office on the literature floor is our library's Special
Collections Research Center, strong in materials relating to
antiquarian books and printing history, radicalism in the arts,
utopian communities, and cartoon and comics history, and with
hundreds of poets represented among the little magazines, rare
books, personal papers, and publisher's archives held there. I spend
my work days generally concerned with our principal collections
and the people who work among them, but always looming above
me is the urge to take the elevator up to spend whatever time I can
immersing myself in the collective aura of the archive.

If there is one poetic impulse that regularly usurps my professional duties as a librarian it is this: I seek to use my position to root through the lives of other poets. I know it will be a career-length endeavor to acquaint myself with the unwieldy, immeasurable expanse of the archive, learning along the way what invisible linkages among the books in our stacks and among the collections in other libraries exist there. To me it is the feeling of frantically assembling a jigsaw puzzle with no edge pieces, and maybe some of the pieces are from another puzzle. And really, where does any good puzzle truly end?

I have learned to employ this impulse in helping patrons and teaching students; I justify the indulgence in academic work about the strategies I use. Every interaction with these collections sets me off on questions I have no time to answer; they live in me and spill out into my work practice and my reading and my interactions with patrons. I've learned that in every box are untold secrets, and in every secret, untold boxes.

Part of me is always trying to reconcile my creative life with my professional life, my work as a librarian with my work as a poet. There is a strong connection between them, but I often have trouble articulating, or perhaps even recognizing it. While I may shift between fully inhabiting either, each is somehow ever-present, listening, searching, noticing, recounting, documenting.

One thing I've noticed about being a librarian working in archival collections is the privilege that comes along with knowing how systems of description and access are supposed to work and how willing other librarians, archivists, curators, and information professionals are to share with me.

It turns out that lots of what I know about our own local archives comes from conversations with the curators, archivists, and others in the reading room; telling stories and listening to stories about our experience in the collections. Despite being a vital part of this work, those conversations are never really present in the apparatus of archival description. But they are alive in the spaces around collections, in the break room, in the elevator; whispered not because they are secrets, but in order not to disturb the other researchers. They feel like secrets.

———

Patrick: I wanted to, quickly, ask if you could just tell me a little bit about your specific job and the kind of questions people ask you?

Tom:[1] Sure, yeah. So my title here is Public Services Specialist, I am sort of second in command in the Public Services Department here, and I do many different things but the way that I interact with the public is that I work our front desk and manage our reading room, and also deal with remote requests like yours.

Patrick: [laughs] OK, cool. I'm glad there are requests like mine. Um, so what type of materials do you handle on a daily basis? Are there things that you're looking at a lot? Or, is it all over the place?

Tom: Yeah, it's different day to day, you know. It's kind of funny actually because, you know, part of the reason that I work here is that I like dealing with the materials, but I really don't get to choose what I get to look at because my time is totally dictated by what other people want to look at [laughs]. So, I'm so busy helping other people, I rarely get to delve into it myself.

Patrick: I know exactly what you mean about ending up kind of dealing with—encountering lots of questions, but just happening to be the one who's there to help other people with it, and not ever knowing what you're going to end up with.

Tom: Right.

———

Recently I led a session for our incoming MFA Creative Writing students; an introduction to some of our literature-related

---

1. Tom McCutchon, Public Services Specialist, Rare Books & Manuscript Library, Columbia University Libraries, interviewed via telephone, June 9, 2016.

special collections, featuring a hard sell on entangling oneself in the constellations of books and documents and ephemera they represent.

Alongside the fancy things like copy Q of Blake's *Songs of Innocence* and our Kelmscott Chaucer, I laid out some more mundane items, things that reflect the actual lives of our writers, things that implicate them in the personal, literary, and business relationships that comprise the machinery of literature. Things like a manuscript of Kathy Acker's *Blood and Guts in High School* (Grove Press, 1984), with a sweet handwritten note to her editor.

Things like a folder of manuscripts from the Leroi Jones (aka Amiri Baraka)[2] Papers of poems from *Yugen* 6[3] including a page with a Robert Creeley poem unceremoniously crossed out. Things like Diane Di Prima's 1966 pocket calendar, noting editorial tasks for *The Floating Bear* and Poet's Press, recipients of letters-to-be-written, dates designated "Cleaning Day," and one marked "New Moon / Buddhist New Year / Druid New Year / LSD." Things like a letter to Grove Press requesting permission to republish portions of *Ficciones*, signed by Jorge Luis Borges.[4]

The poet Brooks Haxton, who teaches at my institution, attended the session, and we both noticed that the young poets and fiction writers in the room seemed almost scared to move, despite having been given permission and training to handle many of the items. Brooks mentioned a Corso poem to me about being struck by the aura of something unique in an archive. I received an email a few days later containing a copy-pasted version of "I Held a Shelley Manuscript."

---

2. LeRoi Jones worked as the Night Librarian at Ramey Air Force Base in Puerto Rico. Imamu Amiri Baraka, *The Autobiography of LeRoi Jones/Amiri Baraka* (New York: Freundlich Books, 1984), 114.

3. *Yugen* is the little magazine that Jones edited from 1958 to 1962. A PDF of issue six may be found here: http://cdn.realitystudio.org/images/bibliographic_bunker/yugen/pdf/yugen.06.pdf

4. He was denied that permission.

A slim folder in the Arna Bontemps Papers (42 linear ft.) contains correspondence between Bontemps, poet and Head Librarian at Fisk University, and Dudley Randall, poet, founder of Broadside Press, and librarian at Eloise Hospital Library and the Wayne County Federated Library.[5] The nineteen letters, which span 1962 to 1967, document a relationship between two men whose poetic and professional lives were quite entangled. The earliest letter involves the submission of some of Randall's poems, along with some written by Margaret Danner, which Randall had typed up, for inclusion in *American Negro Poetry* (Hill and Wang, 1963), edited by Bontemps.

Despite both men being well into their respective library careers at the time, Randall's public career in poetry is in its early stages during these exchanges. It is clear in the reverence and care he takes in the letters that he holds Bontemps in very high esteem— Randall is very formal and comes across as nervous for years. This is exemplified by a telegram Randall transmitted at 7:16 in the morning on Christmas day 1963, to let Bontemps know a local review[6] of *American Negro Poetry* would not be published in advance of Bontemps's upcoming talk in Detroit.

Throughout these letters, the poets discuss the networks of their literary lives, illustrating the dynamics of editor-poet relationships, but the most striking thing to me is the way in which their discourse is embedded in the profession. Bontemps almost always signs his letters with his title (first Head Librarian, later Director of University Relations), and the first letter Randall sent to him (referred to periodically, but not among those in the collection) was an inquiry about a job in the Fisk Library. My favorite piece in the folder is a 1965 hand-written card emblazoned with a portrait of Samuel Coleridge. It begins:

---

5. Julius E. Thompson, *Dudley Randall, Broadside Press, and the Black Arts Movement in Detroit, 1960-1995.* (Jefferson, NC: McFarland & Company), 21.

6. Broadus Butler, "American Negro Poetry: An Enjoyment and a Revelation." *Michigan Chronicle* [Detroit, Michigan] 25 January 1964. Folder 78 of the Bontemps papers contains a clipping of this story.

Dear Mr. Bontemps,

I am Dudley Randall, who once asked you for a job, and who appeared in your *American Negro Poetry.*

I won this stationery from the Gale Research Company, publishers of *Contemporary Authors,* who issued a literary calendar with some blank dates and who offered a packet of literary stationery to anyone who suggested an author's birthdate for any of the blank dates.[7] I looked in their book and found a name for October 13;[8] and thank you for the stationery. (30 May 1965)

Randall goes on to invite Bontemps to visit his monthly poetry workshop when he assumes Bontemps will be in town for the ALA Annual Meeting in Detroit that year. Bontemps replies with delight about the calendar, but with regrets about ALA—he's skipping it that year to attend the PEN International conference, where he will eventually see Arthur Miller be elected the first American president of that organization.

A 1966 letter on the same Gale-supplied stationery (featuring James Fenimore Cooper this time) reveals that Randall and Bontemps met at the historic April 1966 Fisk Black Writers' Conference:[9]

Thank you for your kindness and courtesy to me at the Writer's Conference. I was looking for a place to eat, and you noticed and invited me to sit down at the table. And you invited me to the party after Saunders Riddings' speech. I shan't forget that. (12 May 1966)

The remaining items in the folder document Randall's emergence as a publisher, including a call for submissions to Broadside Press's memorial volume *For Malcolm: Poems on the Life and the Death of Malcolm X,* and, upon the death of Langston Hughes, a request for

---

7. I had eight volumes of *Library Journal* from 1964-1965 delivered to my office to find an announcement of this contest; a couple of hours of searching yielded nothing.

8. Bontemps was born 13 October 1902.

9. Nearly half of the June 1966 issue of *Negro Digest,* which is available in Google Books, is dedicated to the 1966 Fisk Black Writers Conference.

advice regarding royalties for Hughes's "Backlash Blues" broadside, which Randall was in the process of publishing.[10] In these letters, the tone, and even the forms, of Randall's correspondence have shifted from being from a poet writing to his editor to that of a peer and a publisher. The last two items in the folder are Bontemps's personal copies of the first two Broadside Press broadsides, "The Ballad of Birmingham" and "Dressed All in Pink",[11] both written by Randall.

———

Patrick: [laughs] So are there any items that you've encountered either in your career or in your research, that kind of had that effect of sort of stopping your heart, um, you know, things that stick out to you like the one item that had the effect on you that the Shelley manuscript had on Corso?

Tom: [long pause] I don't have instant access to it, so I'm sure I have a better example than the one I'll give you, but I think that . . . Well, a good one is, I got really excited the other day when I was looking through the archives that we recently acquired from Edith Schloss Burckhardt, and she was at one time married to a composer that I really love named Alvin Curran. And he was writing to her—I guess, I'm not sure exactly what time period in their lives that they were married, but the correspondence in her collection is all from a time when he was expatriating for the first time in Rome, and he ended up staying there his whole life. But he was writing her, like, drunk letters.

Patrick: [laughs]

Tom: Writing to her, you know, interacting with her, expressing to her how drunk he is and how much all the people at the party were

10. About which, Randall noted, "I have already listed it in Books in Print 1967." (29 June 1967)

11. The copy of "Dressed All in Pink," a poem following Jackie Kennedy during her husband's assassination, is hand-marked #56 (of 200) in red ink and has a heavy crease near the bottom of the page, I imagine, due to having been sent in a standard-size envelope.

assholes, and just how wild the whole thing is, but mixed with a kind of excitement. Talking about the various events and how the artistic connections are working out for him at a young age and everything. That was really special because it's the sort of thing that I didn't really expect to find here in the archives because it's not really connected to Columbia in any way.

Patrick: Uh huh.

Tom: And, I think it was kind of rare to have this, like, fall in my lap, and it was such an . . . intimate thing and I got to, you know, really see this beautiful moment between two people [laughs]

Patrick: [laughs] Yeah, that sounds great. Is that collection even available yet? Is it being processed? It's new?

Tom: It's available, it's kind of . . . I would call it "minimally processed."

———

From: Patrick Williams (Librarian)[12]
Sent: Monday, September 28, 2015 7:41 AM
To: Brooks Haxton
Subject: RE: Corso

Hi Brooks-
Thanks so much for sending this—I need to find a way to incorporate it into the next session!
As for the actual effects of holding a Shelley manuscript, maybe we should see for ourselves:
http://library.syr.edu/digital/guides/s/shelley_pb.htm[13]
Thanks for coming to the session last week. I hope to do another next fall with different items.

---

12. I'm not the only Patrick Williams at my institution, so I have to append (Librarian) to my email alias in order that correspondence meant for me arrives. It's a constant source of anxiety.

13. The URL of our library's EAD finding aid for the small Shelley collection.

Best,
Patrick

———

Box 1 of the William Van O'Connor Papers (1.7 linear feet) contains twenty-eight folders of correspondence demonstrating the critic, teacher, and poet's broad literary and professional world. The folder marked "1958" holds many letters pertaining to O'Connor's eventual *The New University Wits* (Southern Illinois University Press, 1963), including those penned by its subjects, Iris Murdoch, John Wain, and Kingsley Amis.

As I'm in the reading room thanks to some found time between meetings, I rush through letters by these poets until I arrive at the pale-blue Air Letter I see through the onionskin of the correspondence preceding it. Typed in mock-letterhead at the top of the form: "THE UNIVERSITY AT HULL / THE LIBRARY." It's from Philip Larkin, whom the lead chapter in O'Connor's book features.

In this letter, and many of the others from Larkin in this collection, he is equal parts aloof, tacit, and self-deprecating.[14] O'Connor seeks to know of Larkin's involvement in "The Movement" along his contemporaries Murdoch, Wain, Amis, Donald Davie, and Thom Gunn. Rather than answer questions directly, Larkin refers O'Connor to an article on the topic[15] for answers. He closes the letter:

> I am in fact Librarian of the University of Hull and not any sort of English Teacher. If necessary I could supply a copy of the article I mentioned, but since I have only a very small and diminishing stock of these I should be relieved if you could find a copy or photocopy within the United States. I should be glad to answer any further questions you have. (2 April 1958)

———

14. This approach is continued in Larkin's correspondence regarding a 1982 *Paris Review* interview in our Robert S. Phillips Papers (33 linear feet).

15. "Four Young Poets, I. Philip Larkin." *Times Education Supplement*, 13 July 1956, 931. Larkin does not supply Phillips with the article's title.

In the letters that follow Larkin does exactly that, though he seems very interested in not confirming O'Connor's ideas about the cohesion of the "The Movement." Upon receiving a copy of the book in March 1964, Larkin thanks the author, letting him know he'd already obtained a copy for the library and therefore "what you said of me is not surprising..." He goes on:

> Looking back at our correspondence in 1958 (yes, I still have it) I am rather ashamed of my somewhat laconic replies to your requests for information, but I suppose I was brought up to think that it is better to say too little than too much. (24 March 1964)

Even in literary conversations, Larkin seems to draw more authority and legitimacy from his professional work. Eventually, O'Connor is granted a one-year teaching placement at Hull, and Larkin helps to secure him housing. In Larkin's condolence letter to O'Connor's widow Mary the following year, he foregrounds their professional, rather than literary, relationship:

> I particularly remember him as a genial and friendly colleague, whom one always felt better for having seen, and who was graciously tolerant of our many short-comings as a University. I was also grateful for the attention he had given to the few things I have written. It is good to know that you enjoyed your year here, and I am sure that we all retain very happy memories of your visit. (20 December 1966)

I present these findings as a work in progress at a campus archival research symposium, after being introduced to the audience as a librarian. I neglect to mention that I'm also a poet.

Scope and Contents of the Collection[16]

The Percy Bysshe Shelley Collection consists of one fragment in Shelley's hand and three letters concerning him. The letter from

----

16. From the finding aid for the Percy Bysshe Shelley Collection, http://library. syr.edu/digital/guides/s/shelley_pb.htm

Percy Florence Shelley, dated 14 Nov 1883, contains comments about his father's vegetarianism. Of the letters from Jane, Lady Shelley, one contains remarks on an article about Shelley published in the *National Review* and the other expresses gratitude to the recipient (unnamed) for his "understanding of [Shelley's] character."

Poet-librarian Audre Lorde appears briefly in the papers of Arna Bontemps. In 1966 she wrote Bontemps inquiring about the planned new edition of *Poetry of the Negro* (Doubleday, 1970), and offered poems. In the letter, she mentions that her work had appeared on the syllabus for a class at Teachers' College at Columbia University. Bontemps responds with an invitation for Lorde to submit, and mentions he'd also consider the work Langston Hughes had published by Lorde in *New Negro Poets: USA* (Indiana University Press, 1964). In a letter sent along with her submission, Lorde, then thirty-two, requests that Bontemps pay closest attention to her more recent work, as the poems appearing in *New Negro Poets* were written when she was in high school.

No poems of Lorde's appear in *Poetry of the Negro*; a rejection.

Lorde is sadly absent from our Diane di Prima Papers (2.5 linear feet), despite the close friendship they maintained. In Lorde's first collection, *The First Cities* (Poets' Press, 1968), di Prima provides the introduction, revealing that:

> I have known Audre Lorde since we were fifteen, when we read our poems to each other in front of our Home Room at Hunter High school. And only two months ago, she delivered my child.
>
> A woman's world, peopled with men & children and the dead, exotic as scallops.

In our copy, di Prima has signed and dated this page May 14, 1987, which for some reason, I run my finger over.

Though (non-librarian) poet Gregory Corso is present though poems and letters in no fewer than five collections in my institution's special collections, our small Gregory Corso Collection only contains four items from 1961: outgoing letters to Marshall Bean and Richard Meltzer, a typescript of Corso's collection *Long Live Man* (New Directions, 1962), and a notebook with "Long Live Man" written in pencil on the cover. "I Held a Shelley Manuscript" appeared in Corso's previous book, *The Happy Birthday of Death*, so I was a bit curious to see whether there was any trace of it in that notebook.

There was not.

But while reading the typed letter Corso wrote to Marshall Bean from Athens, I copied down a single line: "and lo! yr letter hit me hard." "God I hope you ain't dead Marshall" is scrawled in blue ballpoint at the bottom of the page.

———

I'm holding a Shelley manuscript. I came across it accidentally as I was preparing for a class on local social justice archives, and it just happened to be in the same box. When I saw "Percy Bysshe Shelley Collection" on the folder tab, I couldn't quite catch my breath.

But I quickly regained it on opening the folder.

To call it a fragment is perhaps too generous. It's about an inch and a half tall and five inches wide, clearly excised from a larger prose document. It is ungrand. Maybe it has fourteen words, but I can barely make them out. Is it French? "1818" is penciled in beneath the script. The ink is tan, as in Corso's observation, but the page is not fragile. It's been pasted and (and at some time matted) to card stock, with a scar of old adhesive underscoring its torn lower edge.

———

Patrick: So, I just wanted to let you know I'm sitting here with a copy of the poem that I printed out from a screenshot of the [Google Books preview version] of *Mindfield*, which is at least the third time the poem was republished in a book. So I'm looking at a really different copy than the one you looked at.

Tom: Yeah, I've got it in front of me right now actually.

Patrick: Oh really! [laughs]

Tom: There's actually two versions in this folder.

Patrick: Oh, wow!

Tom: One is a typewritten manuscript that he signed on onionskin, and the other one looks like it's an edited version.

Patrick: Do you have any connection to Shelley or Corso? In terms of what you've studied or what you're interested in?

Tom: Well, I was an English major in college, so, you know to some extent yes. But neither of them are intimates of mine.

Patrick: Got it. Ok, so can you tell me what you thought of the poem, just briefly?

Tom: Well, I thought that it was, you know, I know Corso was a Beat, or associated with them, and I always appreciate the economy of their writing and the emotion that they pack in to it, so that was nice. Looking at the manuscript, it was interesting to see how some of the edits made such a big difference.

Patrick: Uh huh

Tom: Particularly with punctuation. Because I think that the final, well I'm not comparing this to a final one, obviously, but the more polished version has much more punctuation.

Patrick: Oh.

Tom: The other one has no punctuation. That was quite interesting because it kind of changes things. The earlier version—I also just tend to like earlier versions of things in general. [laughs] Yeah, I can relate to the feeling that he's got here. Just the sheer excitement of being able to connect with this item and the person through the item.

Patrick: Yeah! So you've already mentioned some of the things you've noticed about it, but are there other things you notice besides the differences between the versions, anything about the paper, or marking, or what have been involved other than the typewriters in their production?

Tom: Yeah, you know the onionskin is always a nice touch in this time period. You know it was more common in that period. I was born in '83, so it was never even commonplace for me. His—I'm guessing that it's his own edits—are here in red ink—I'll send you a picture of it—but he's got some formatting in some just really crude red ink that's childish and smearing and I feel like that's very endearing. The poem itself too, I think, increasingly becomes—the whole thing is kind of this affected tone, and gets more and more so as it goes on, which I guess is a testament to how much he's affected by the manuscript.

Patrick: Uh huh.

Tom: I don't know—it's neat that I'm wondering why he signed it.

Patrick: Does it remind you of anything? Like any other pieces, collections, items that you've seen?

Tom: Does it remind me of anything? Hmmm. Well, the thing that it reminds me of is sort of a non sequitur in a way, um, because, you know, all of these things kind of start to look similar after a while.

Patrick: Uh huh.

Tom: But, the interesting thing about it maybe is that what it reminds me of immediately is: a lot of times with the handwritten manuscripts, or correspondence, you have the version that is on the parchment or whatever, kind of more cloudy looking document, and then, you know, probably very difficult to read. Both of these [typed pages] are not so much this case, but then a lot of times you'll have, you know, some academic has gone through it and leaves their typed translation of it to make things easier on some future academic.

Patrick: Yeah.

Tom: And they're placed next to it. And that's what this is kind of immediately reminding me of.

Patrick: [laughs]

Tom: Having the cleaned up version right next to the other one, like maybe you couldn't understand the intent of what he was doing there.

Patrick: Yeah, and I imagine there is a handwritten version of this—I think it might be in some notebooks that are at UNC Chapel Hill—I haven't found out yet—because you can't imagine that he had a typewriter in there in the reading room while he was writing. [laughs]

Tom: Yeah, probably not. And the kind of drafty version on the typewriter also at the bottom says "Printed in OXFORD MAGAZINE" and "gregory corso" and then he signed it.

Patrick: Oh yeah, yeah, I feel like I see that a lot.

Tom: So it's kind of—I'm not sure why he would have re-typed it, what purpose.

Patrick: You said there was some red ink—are there any sort of traces of, you know, Corso's body on it? Are there marks, or smudges?

Tom: [laughs] Yeah, totally. It looks like you know kind of the way a smudgy eraser marks up a page. Multiple marks like that. I don't know where they are from, but they are like the size of an eraser tip all over the page.

Patrick: Hmm.

———

The John Wieners Papers (0.75 linear feet) contains items relating to the poet, who once worked in the Lamont Library at Harvard,[17] covering the period of 1955 to 1970. In it are a handful of correspondence files,[18] some clippings and fliers, and manuscripts and production files for his collection *Ace of Pentacles* (Phoenix Books, 1964). It also contains photocopies of the three issues of *Measure*, the little magazine that Wieners edited, and various other writings, including a small notepad advertising the Atlantic Pipe & Supply Co., Inc., of Boston. It's a very compact collection, but I've returned to it often because it is dense with surprises.

In one letter, Marianne Moore (who worked in the New York Public Library's Hudson Park Branch[19] from 1921-1925[20]) graciously declines to send Wieners poems for the second issue of *Measure*.

17. Raymond Foye, "John Wieners," in *The Beats: Literary Bohemians in Postwar American (Dictionary of Literary Bibliography* Volume 16 Part 2), ed. Ann Charters (Detroit: Gale Research Company, 1983), 572-583.

18. Including a letter from Archibald MacLeish, poet and ninth Librarian of Congress.

19. My dear friend Miranda Murray became the manager of this branch library in 2013, and is quite proud of the Moore association: "We have a plaque!"

20. Richard Macksey, "Marianne (Craig) Moore: A Brief Chronology," in *Marianne Moore: A Collection of Critical Essays*, ed. Charles Tomlinson (Englewood Cliffs, NJ: Prentice Hall, 1969), 179-181.

But she thanks him for sending her the first issue, and excitedly quotes from the Charles Olson and Jack Spicer poems it contains. The Spicer poem, "Song for Bird and Myself," concerns two birds who have found their way into a Rare Book Room[21] like the one I sit in as I read from the thick and grainy sixties mimeo. For some reason, I prefer these ghostly surrogates to the actual copies sitting on my cart fifteen feet away.

Even Corso's in there, asking for poems from Wieners for *Junge Amerikanische Lyrik* (Hanser, 1961), an anthology he co-edited with Walter Höllerer, and requesting copies of *Measure* and *Evergreen Review* to be sent to him care of American Express in Venice.

The notepad, which I have also returned to often, stopped my heart the first time I saw it. As I flipped through it, I experienced a feeling I've only had when dealing with priceless or fragile items—I was scared. The small cardboard cover features the dents and smudges one would expect from something kept so close to a body. To *his* body. What it contains feels so deeply personal: "I am miserable / but this misery I have to endure / It is what the gods demand of me," lines written on the train, political poems, poems of erotic desire and action, and the addresses and phone numbers of fellow poets and acquaintances. About halfway through the notepad, Wieners works out the zodiac in diagrams and notes:

Jupiter in Leo gives people
big hearts.
. . .
Mars in the 12th could lead
to surgery.
. . .
Capricorn's a politician's sign.

Another page features only three words in Wiener's gentle script:

Holy love affairs

---

21. Spicer himself worked in the Rare Book Room at the Boston Public Library in 1955-6. Michael Davidson, "Jack Spicer," in *The Beats: Literary Bohemians in Postwar American* (*Dictionary of Literary Bibliography* Volume 16 Part 2), ed. Ann Charters (Detroit: Gale Research Company, 1983), 511-517.

I delete the images I take of these pages, and photograph them again when I return.

———

Patrick: Did you look at anything else in that box?

Tom: I didn't, no. I just went right for that one.

Patrick: Yeah, it seems like that finding aid is so, like, detailed, and looks like a really well-organized collection.

Tom: Yeah, it's unusual, actually. It's nice when you have that. It didn't lead me to wander.

Patrick: Is there anything about handling these two pages that is different from what you normally do?

Tom: Well I guess the thing that's different about it is just simply the fact that I had the space to think a little bit more creatively— sometimes you get seized by something and you'll just kind of create a little extra time for it, but given the nature of your request I did at least, you know, read and open myself up to it a little bit more.

Patrick: [laughs]

Tom: Whereas normally, I'm kind of just very purpose driven, and trying to get it done quickly.

Patrick: Yeah.

Tom: And move on to the next thing.

Patrick: I can imagine. So, does handling it make you—I'll reference the poem here—does handling it make you feel anything? [laughs] I guess I'm asking, um, did your hands numb to beauty?

Tom: [laughs] I guess you could say so. I think any time that I handle something that somebody else touched from another period, particularly something that's creative, you feel a little bit like you just eavesdropped on that person or peeked in their window or something. Or, for like a second, you were that person or something; like, you're seeing it through their eyes. That's a really cool feeling, always. It's funny because most of the time, you know, in these people's archives, you get so excited that you found a letter from whoever to whoever, and both are such interesting people, and then you read the letter and it's like, it's nothing. There's nothing to it, but you still feel so privileged to have eavesdropped on their little conversation. It feels so significant, but they're just talking about, "it was nice to see you the other day." [laughs]

Patrick: All right. I just have one last question, which isn't really a question. Do you know where Corso's ashes are buried?

Tom: I don't, no.

Patrick: They buried them right in front of Percy Shelley's grave in Rome.

Tom: Ah ha.

Patrick: I thought that was kind of special.

Tom: Yeah, that is.

Collections consulted:
Arna Bontemps Papers, Diane Di Prima Papers, Gregory Corso Collection, Grove Press Records, John Wieners Papers, Leroi Jones (aka Amiri Baraka) Papers, Percy Bysshe Shelley Collection, Robert S. Phillips Papers, William Van O'Connor Papers, Special Collections Research Center, Syracuse University Libraries.

The author is grateful for the assistance of Michele Coombs, Kelly Delevan, Nicole Westerdahl, Nicolette Dobrowolski, Brooks Haxton, Tom McCutchon, Sean Quimby, and the entire staff of the Special Collections Research Center at the Syracuse University Libraries.

Bibliography

Baraka, Imamu Amiri. *The Autobiography of LeRoi Jones / Amiri Baraka*. New York, NY: Freundlich Books, 1984. 114.

Butler, Broadus. "American Negro Poetry: An Enjoyment and a Revelation." *Michigan Chronicle* [Detroit, Michigan] 25 January 1964.

Davidson, Michael. "Jack Spicer." In *The Beats: Literary Bohemians in Postwar American (Dictionary of Literary Bibliography* Volume 16 Part 2), edited by Ann Charters, 511-17. Detroit: Gale Research Company, 1983.

"Four Young Poets, I. Philip Larkin." *Times Education Supplement*, 13 July 1956. 931.

Foye, Raymond. "John Wieners." In *The Beats: Literary Bohemians in Postwar American (Dictionary of Literary Bibliography* Volume 16 Part 2), edited by Ann Charters, 572-83. Detroit: Gale Research Company, 1983. 572-583. Print.

Macksey, Richard. "Marianne (Craig) Moore: A Brief Chronology." In *Marianne Moore: A Collection of Critical Essays*, edited by Charles Tomlinson, 179 181. Englewood Cliffs, NJ: Prentice Hall, 1969.

Thompson, Julius E. *Dudley Randall, Broadside Press, and the Black Arts Movement in Detroit, 1960-1995*. Jefferson, NC: McFarland & Company, 2005.

Williams, Patrick. Interview with Tom McCutchon. Personal interview. New York, June 9, 2016.

Yugen 6. Ed. Amiri Baraka. http://cdn.realitystudio.org/images/ bibliographic_bunker/yugen/pdf/yugen.06.pdf

Moonburn City

Patrick Williams

You've heard taxi radios crackle the busted polyrhythms
of at least a dozen hidden cities the further you get from downtown.
We now know that everyone was a Quincy punk, including me,
including M. Curie of Plutonia. Her cookbooks still glow
at night, when the archives are all locked up. Right this moment
only your arm is still in the room, and even it's just here
to turn out the light. Remember, it took an astronomer to teach you
not to stare into the sun. Why am I so jealous of your childhood
dream, the one that ended with that hatchet sailing toward
your face? While you were sleeping, I was out in the shed,
sawing stolen shotgun shells. Back then, my favorite advice
was to just get high and maybe watch *Tokyo Olympiad* again.
Our teledata weakens at the treeline, I'm told, caught in the fading
goldenrod grids of every April cafeteria lunch. The type is set
in double undermine. The food is subpar, even the descriptions
are no fun at all. Let's remember. Let's confess. Let's unpack
every memory of leaving, of the bravest kind of quitting:
so early or so late. Let's forget real light and glow. Of course
I know what machismo is. I learned it from that song.

Chapter 12

SCHOLARLY COMMUNICATION, BUREAUCRACY, DARKNESS AND DESIRE: POETS IN THE AGE OF THE QUANTIFIED SELF

Aaron McCollough

Yesterday, a colleague told me she firmly believed everything in the world could be quantified. I wanted to be accommodating and professional, and I felt obliged to act like I thought this was a reasonable thing to believe. In fact, however, something had suddenly caught fire somewhere inside my skull. I had to swill the entire contents of my Nalgene bottle just to slow the burning. And, as everyone knows, most fire deaths are caused not by burns but by smoke inhalation. I laughed in the wrong way.

No, she was emphatic, *everything* can be accurately accounted for and explained with numeric data. I wanted to get into arguing about ontology — by "everything that is" did she mean to include metaphysics? — but there was so much smoke now. We all had to crawl out of the office, and as we were crawling, we had to agree to disagree.

I'm a scholarly communications librarian. Like so many areas of librarianship ("information literacy," "area studies"), "scholarly communications" sounds like it could be describing anything, everything, or nothing done in libraries. For example,

Christin Wixson recently summarized it thus: "the term 'scholarly communication' refers to all the processes involved in the creation, dissemination, use and stewardship of knowledge related to research and teaching."[1] Hm. She's right, of course, but substitute "information literacy" or "area studies" for "scholarly communication" in the first clause and I'm not sure anything changes – not, at least, for anyone outside the library. This is a problem with jargon, of course, and it's by no means unique to libraries. But libraries are often abstractly imagined to be bastions of organizational rectitude and clarity. They are inhabited by people who believe everything can be quantified. What does it mean when the labels libraries use to describe their own work are illegible to their patrons and even to themselves?

One reasonable answer might be something like this: academic budgetary structures and knowledge infrastructures are being transformed in unprecedentedly rapid ways and in ways that are inconsistently distributed across institutions. In an effort to adapt, libraries have been continually introducing pilot services and shoehorning them into the broadest possible categories. These categories are akin to what Wallace Stevens called "necessary fictions":

> If when the primacy of the intelligence has been achieved, one can really say what a man is actually like, what could be more natural than a science of illusions? Moreover, if the imagination is not quite the clue to reality now, might it not become so then? As for the present, what have we, if we do not have science, except the imagination? And who is to say of its deliberate fictions arising out of the contemporary mind that they are not the forerunners of some such science?[2]

In lieu of having achieved the "primacy of intelligence," or the end of history, trapped as we are in the present, these "deliberate

---

1. Christin Wixson, "Scholarly Communication Services at Plymouth State University: A Feasibility Report," Plymouth State University, March 7, 2016.

2. Wallace Stevens, *The Necessary Angel; Essays on Reality and the Imagination* (New York: Knopf, 1951), 139.

fictions arising out of the contemporary mind" enable us to aim at addressing the murky obligations of an emergent "new reality" while continuing to do the traditional work whose necessity did not pass with the "old reality." Following this trend of thought, we might be tempted to say that librarians are like the female singer/ maker at the center of Stevens' famous "The Idea of Order at Key West":

> when she sang, the sea,
> Whatever self it had, became the self
> That was her song, for she was the maker. Then we,
> As we beheld her striding there alone,
> Knew that there never was a world for her
> Except the one she sang and, singing, made. [ll. 38-43]

In our "rage for order," are we not doing creative and transformative work, making the world that we are ostensibly singing about and singing about the world that we are ostensibly making? By this logic, might not the baggy categories we use to describe our new functions be the "forerunners to some . . . science?" Perhaps. But let's hold this thought for further consideration below.

Of course, scholarly communication librarians like me work on specific kinds of things most of the day, and it is sometimes easier to think of the work in practical terms via "service models." Focusing in this way risks overlooking the big picture and the considerable labor (traditional and emotional) we dedicate to driving institutional change. But, in my rage for order, I'll take this as an acceptable risk, at least for the moment. We scholarly communications folk maintain institutional repositories, which at bottom usually entails a set of project-management tasks, but which can also include metadata creation and scripting in a variety of programming languages. We offer a range of copyright services, which means we have to know a great deal about copyright, and which also means we have to find a way to give trustworthy guidance without giving "legal advice." Many of us are involved in offering some form of library publishing services (especially online journal hosting and coordination, but increasingly digitally "networked" books, as well), which means we need to know something, preferably a lot, about an extremely diverse business with its own legacy of traditions, prejudices, and best-practices. Many of us also coordinate the logistics and communications associated with Open Access policy compliance (local, federal, and independent-funder), which includes (as most of the above services do) a range of service-tailored outreach and instruction efforts. Finally, we are increasingly finding ourselves in charge of establishing "faculty profile services" or "current research information systems."

This last set of tools and services, maybe due to its novelty, seems the most inchoate. On the face of it, a faculty profile service appears simple enough. By creating a central database of all faculty achievements (especially publications), such a system could serve as a stable, systematic portal for conveying a university's research identity. It's not hard to imagine some innocuous benefits to such a system: a way-finding tool for students, would-be collaborators, and even media outlets. Especially in a large, distributed university environment (imagine state systems like California or North Carolina, for example), the basic task of accurately representing the collective scholarly achievements and the full range of local expertise is a tremendous one. But it's also a task that seems worth trying to tackle, and this feels like the kind of organizational work libraries would be well suited to handling in a Stevensesque "new reality."

There is, however, an undeniably creepy dimension to all of this, skulking in the shadows cast by questions about quantification—not solely its limits, but also its potential reach. Libraries have traditionally practiced a variety of measuring functions. Library self-assessment measures, like gate counts and circulation statistics, have primarily been designed to capture an impression of collection and services usage, but by extension these have offered only a fairly vague sense of campus research activity. The rise of networked information has enabled increasingly powerful bibliometric techniques and forms of citation and circulation analysis. So, some combination of inertia and well-meaning utilitarianism is probably enough to explain the naturalness librarians like me have found in the progress of profiling systems into our suite of offerings. We like collecting, arranging, and counting things, and we're here to help the faculty and the university collect, arrange, and count the things they value. No problem.

As long as what we're really talking about is librarians collecting, owning, and meting out this information, maybe there isn't a problem. Especially in libraries with powerful faculty governance structures, one can imagine these activities being guided by a clear set of policies that guarantee ethical practice and rigorous oversight. It might still seem a little creepy to some faculty members, and the question of quantification's limits persists, but one can at least imagine a world where these data, owned by the academy and curated by its libraries, would be used virtuously. This imaginary world, I think, is the one I have been taking for granted in the initial development of the local infrastructure on my campus.

But these things take time. And recent developments in the marketplace (plus deeper study on my couch) have forced me to contemplate a less ideal future. First, on May 17, 2016, the Dutch publishing behemoth Elsevier purchased SSRN, the Social Science Research Network. SSRN is a pre-print server, meaning it has long served as a digital deposit and access repository for scholarly papers in "pre-print" form (i.e., the author's manuscript before typesetting and copyediting done by a publisher). Since 1994, SSRN has been a desirable place for scholars to seek wide readership via a *gratis* open-access model. The Elsevier purchase came as a surprise to many. As Christopher Kelty pointed out, however, SSRN's real commodity value was not in the articles it hosted, but in the data its systems collected about researcher behavior. The SSRN user data quality is very high:

> All models are wrong, but some are useful. SSRN represents better data about the impact of social science research than any single journal, or any publisher's data (even Elsevier, with its hundreds of social science journals), because it has been built on the good

will, apparent neutrality, and level playing field of an open access repository.

And high-quality data demonstrating research "impact" is a currency that cannot be easily coined:

> Academic administrators long ago gave up evaluating scholars based on quality or innovative research, and turned to evaluating "impact" instead. And impact is a sort of metaphysical quality that is not in the research itself, but in the circulation and reception of research—it can only be captured by metrics, which requires collecting data. The reason is obvious to anyone who works in the university: impact = higher rankings, higher rankings = more and better students, more donors, more reputation for the institution . . . all of which translates into the ability to hire more high impact researchers. If that kind of data is valuable to academic administrators, Elsevier is right to focus on collecting more if it, monetizing it, and selling it back to Universities.[3]

Elsevier is wisely looking to diversify its business model in the face of rising pressure to convert toll-access journal literature to open access. Taking advantage of a system that has long treated fuzzy categories of prestige, brand, and reputational capital as proxy measures for quality, they are following their tested strategy of monopolizing high-value information streams into a new era.

Even more recently, the University of Florida Library announced it was moving into the second phase of an Institutional Repository pilot project with Elsevier to "maximize visibility, impact, and dissemination of research articles by UF Authors."[4] Citing a local researcher culture "that has not been one to embrace author deposit," Library Dean Judith Russell explained that UF research publications appear in Elsevier journals with significantly

---

3. Christopher M. Kelty, "It's the Data, Stupid: What Elsevier's Purchase of SSRN Also Means," *Savage Minds,* May 18, 2016, http://savageminds.org/2016/05/18/its-the-data-stupid-what-elseviers-purchase-of-ssrn-also-means/.

4. Barbara Hood and Sacha Boucherie, "University of Florida and Elsevier Collaborate to Maximize Visibility, Impact and Dissemination of Research Articles by UF Authors," Elsevier, May 19, 2016.

higher frequency than with other publishers.[5] The new project uses Elsevier's ScienceDirect APIs to populate the IR@UF institutional repository with metadata from and links to Elsevier-hosted content. Independent journalist Richard Poynder referred to the announcement of the relationship as "Elsevier begins to co-opt the institutional repository,"[6] and he's not wrong. Much of the value this arrangement provides Elsevier is fairly obvious. It gives them a deep toehold in a campus digital archive, while pushing library users to Elsevier systems and Elsevier content. This streamlines UF researcher usage data for Elsevier content by capturing preprint usage alongside "final version" usage. And, should they prove successful in penetrating multiple large Institutional Repositories, the enhanced, networked dataset would grow exponentially more valuable with each new addition.

The benefit to the library is not immediately or completely clear. Who cares if UF researchers have not embraced author deposit? This is a widespread phenomenon, and it has undermined much of the early enthusiasm for "green open access," but populating an Institutional Repository with metadata and links to paywalled content does nothing to remedy that problem. In theory, IR@UF users might benefit from an improved discovery experience, but as has been demonstrated, STEM researchers don't typically rely on library resources for this purpose.[7] More likely, the promise of benefit lies in "consolidated article impact metrics as well as standardized usage reporting" (the fourth benefit promised on Elsevier's "Enhancing repository services" page).[8] As noted by Kelty, these are the kind of data Elsevier is keen to collect, monetize, and sell back to universities as a value-added service. As

5. Judith Russell, "Re: UF-Elsevier Pilot Project," Coalition of Open Access Policy Institutions, May 23, 2016, sparc-coapi@sparcopen.org.

6. Richard Poynder, Twitter post, May 26, 2016, https://twitter.com/RickyPo/status/735844228312510464.

7. Roger C. Schonfeld, *Does Discovery Still Happen in the Library?: Roles and Strategies for a Shifting Reality*, Ithaka S+R, September 24, 2014.

8. Elsevier, "Enhancing Repository Services at Your Institution," accessed May 30, 2016, Elsevier, https://www.elsevier.com/solutions/sciencedirect/support/institutional-repository.

an early adopter, perhaps UF can avoid paying for this service for a longer time than others.

I'm personally less concerned about the balance of costs and benefits here between a library and publisher than I am about the general trend of the calculus sizing up as its backdrop. There are many ways of naming it: "audit culture," "new managerialism," "Taylorism," "academic capitalism," etc. I prefer to call it "quantifying the self."

As a poet in the library, a scholarly communications librarian who is also a poet, I'm becoming increasingly concerned that much of my work has been done in service of a system I've misunderstood but which ultimately reifies a set of values I reject. This, it seems, is one of the dangers inherent to relying on "necessary fictions" in professional life—you are likely not their author. As with most things in modern life, their author is probably capital.

Financial challenges in higher education are not new. The arts and humanities have been suffering from crises and cuts for my entire adult life. Nevertheless, the twenty-first century—especially the era of austerity kicked off by the 2008 global financial recession—has witnessed the rise of an unprecedented strain of neo-liberal pressure to justify educational activities according to economic values. I think the discourse of "impact" is a fraud. I believe the wholesale application of market logic to the administration of higher education is not about accountability but ideological interpellation. As a poet in the library, I need to resist this process and to help others resist it. But, how do I do that without shirking my responsibilities? Bureaucracy does have positive values, too, and rebelling virtuously is not a simple undertaking.

Lately, when I've gotten down, I've turned to this passage from Rebecca Solnit:

> The tyranny of the quantifiable is partly the failure of language and discourse to describe more complex, subtle, and fluid phenomena, as well as the failure of those who shape opinions and make decisions to understand and value these slipperier things. It is difficult, sometimes even impossible, to value what cannot be

named or described, and so the task of naming and describing is an essential one in any revolt against the status quo of capitalism and consumerism. Ultimately the destruction of the Earth is due in part, perhaps in a large part, to a failure of the imagination or to its eclipse by systems of accounting that can't count what matters. The revolt against this destruction is a revolt of the imagination, in favor of subtleties, of pleasures money can't buy and corporations can't command, of being producers rather than consumers of meaning, of the slow, the meandering, the digressive, the exploratory, the numinous, the uncertain.[9]

Solnit's remarkable affirmation of indeterminacy is the product of a meditation on an even more remarkable assertion from Virginia Woolf: "the future is dark, which is the best thing the future can be, I think." Woolf's idea, as Solnit notes, is that uncertainty matters; it's generative, essential, unassailable. Not knowing, not being able to know. Letting go of the urge to control, giving in to something at once more basic and also more mysterious. Solnit refers to this basic thing as "[revolt of] the meandering, the digressive, the exploratory, the numinous, the uncertain." She notes that Woolf's formulation is akin to others expressed by Whitman and Rimbaud ("I contain multitudes," "Je est un autre"), and, especially, by Keats ("Negative Capability ... when a man is capable of being in uncertainties ... without any irritable reaching after fact and reason").

In the library, we are often more inclined to stabilize, pin down, flatten, and otherwise "preserve" the objects of our work, and that has made a fair amount of sense for books, a knowledge-infrastructure tool we understand pretty well. But, as Solnit points out, the world—the full envelope of "what matters"—resists this kind of preservation. Indeed, to preserve things in this way often requires the killing of the same things. This may help explain the dubiety of the necessary fictions we've so far concocted in areas like mine.

---

9. Rebecca Solnit, "Woolf's Darkness: Embracing the Inexplicable," *New Yorker*, April 24, 2014.

"In Wildness," Thoreau says, "is the preservation of the World." A poet in the library should not be a taxidermist.

In the face of all this—bureaucracy's holding cells and scales, its arrogance and its capacity to facilitate order and, sometimes, even justice—I'm inclined to say, "in preservation is the wildness of the world." A less romantic emphasis, perhaps, than Thoreau's, but I don't think it's the most glum way of thinking about my work.

Far from Steven's singer/maker bending external reality to the new reality of her song (what Keats would have called a product of "the egotistical sublime"), I'm still not innocent of self-flattering literary identifications. I've already compared myself to Virginia Woolf, Walt Whitman, Arthur Rimbaud, and Henry David Thoreau! Allow me one more.

I flatter myself by imagining the poet in the library as a relative of the Deleuzian Joseph K. As Réda Bensmaïa describes this *Gaya Scienza* of Kafka's work, "Kafka knew that to find justice—the justice he was seeking, that traversed him—it was necessary to move, to go from one room to another, from office to office, from language to language, and from country to country, always following his desire."[10] This "immanent quest following the line of infinite flight" just gets richer and weirder the more diabolically encoded our information practice becomes. In the context of such preservation and wildness, who better than a poet to look for emergencies, excrescences, escape hatches, off-beat songs?

---

10. Réda Bensmaïa, "Preface: The Kafka Effect," In *Kafka: Toward a Minor Literature*, by Gilles Deleuze and Félix Guattari, translated by Dana Polan (Minneapolis, MN: University of Minnesota Press, 1985), xxi.

Bibliography

Bensmaïa, Réda. "Preface: The Kafka Effect." In *Kafka: Toward a Minor Literature, by Gilles Deleuze and Félix Guattari*, translated by Dana Polan, ix-xxi. Minneapolis, MN: University of Minnesota Press, 1985.

Elsevier. "Enhancing Repository Services at Your Institution." Elsevier. Accessed May 30, 2016. https://www.elsevier. com/solutions/sciencedirect/support/institutional-repository.

Hood, Barbara, and Sacha Boucherie. "University of Florida and Elsevier Collaborate to Maximize Visibility, Impact and Dissemination of Research Articles by UF Authors. " Elsevier, May 19, 2016. https://www.elsevier.com/about/ press-releases/science-and-technology/university-of-florida-and-elsevier-collaborate-to-maximize-visibility,-impact-and-dissemination-of-research-articles-by-uf-authors.

Kelty, Christopher M. "It's the Data, Stupid: What Elsevier's Purchase of SSRN Also Means." *Savage Minds*, May 18, 2016. http://savageminds.org/2016/05/18/its-the-data-stupid-what-elseviers-purchase-of-ssrn-also-means/.

Poynder, Richard. "Elsevier begins . . ." Twitter post. May 26, 2016. https://twitter.com/RickyPo/ status/735844228312510464

Russell, Judith. "Re: UF-Elsevier Pilot Project." Coalition of Open Access Policy Institutions, May 23, 2016. sparc-coapi@sparcopen.org.

Schonfeld, Roger C. *Does Discovery Still Happen in the Library? Roles and Strategies for a Shifting Reality.* Ithaka S+R. September 24, 2014.

Solnit, Rebecca. "Woolf's Darkness: Embracing the Inexplicable." *New Yorker*, April 24, 2014. http://www.newyorker.com/ books/page-turner/woolfs-darkness-embracing-the- inexplicable.

Stevens, Wallace. *The Necessary Angel; Essays on Reality and the Imagination*. New York: Knopf, 1951.

Wixson, Christin. "Scholarly Communication Services at Plymouth State University: A Feasibility Report." Plymouth State University, March 7, 2016.

10/8/16

Aaron McCollough

since the wilderness slipped
was columbus
stealing from a flowery hill
as cloud's shadow
the dark fleet of sedans
ready in the rain

does your west hurt you now
sun setting penumbra drawn

the fruit suspended in net
masked by the hole in your eye

love stays not at noon
tilts with the body

does your west hurt you now
who would now recline

Chapter 13

THE GRANTING OF GRACE IN AN ORDINARY ROOM

Shannon Tharp

My earliest memory of the library is located in the Big Horn County Public Library in Basin, Wyoming. My grandmother worked there in a variety of roles, as one does in a rural library, for many years. I remember visiting her and hunting for books. I loved being left to my own devices, left to just be. I was allowed to feel my way around, all instinct. This is also my earliest memory of serendipitous discovery: the act of encountering valuable information when not directly looking for it.

There are theories of information behavior that airily try to encapsulate serendipitous discovery, scholarly articles in which serendipitous discovery is portrayed as a risky tool that stands in opposition to the majority of discovery now taking place online. How can libraries remain vital when patrons are still physically browsing the stacks? How can we capitalize on the future's future? How can we avoid being called old-fashioned?

To want time, wholly unengineered, among the materials in a library isn't strange or passé. Time spent looking, time spent listening, time spent aided only by your capable brain—all that, too, is viable. Still. All that, too, is work.

———

In a 2012 *Paris Review* interview Maureen McLane, an excellent poet, talks with Susan Howe, an excellent poet:

> **McLane**: Do you think of the work you do in libraries and archives as research? As telepathy? As spelunking?
>
> **Howe**: Because of my outsider status—until 1988, when I went to SUNY Buffalo as a visiting fellow—gaining access to the stacks of a university library has always seemed to me an adventure verging on trespass . . . What I love about university libraries is that they always seem slightly off-limits, therefore forbidden. I feel I've been allowed in with my little identity card and now I'm going to be bad. I have the sense of lurking rather than looking. You came in search of a particular volume, but right away you feel the pull of others.[1]

Howe then quotes Emily Dickinson's "Luck is not chance" (1350), here in full:

> Luck is not chance –
> It's Toil –
> Fortune's expensive smile
> Is earned –
> The Father of the Mine
> Is that old-fashioned Coin
> We spurned –

———

I want to know of other poems in which Emily Dickinson used "luck." Here in 2017, I can visit the Emily Dickinson Archive online[2] and attempt a search for the word. In doing so, I find luck in one other poem: "My Portion is Defeat – today – " (639). I turn to my copy of Thomas H. Johnson's *The Complete Poems of Emily*

---

1. Maureen McLane, "Susan Howe, The Art of Poetry No. 97," *Paris Review*, Winter 2012, accessed October 20, 2016, http://www.theparisreview.org/interviews/6189/susan-howe-the-art-of-poetry-no-97-susan-howe.

2. "Emily Dickinson Archive," Harvard University Press, accessed December 23, 2016, http://www.edickinson.org/.

Dickinson[3] to look at 639 in person, so to speak. There's luck, in the poem's second line:

> My Portion is Defeat – today –
> A paler luck than Victory –

In making my way to poem 639, page 316, I noticed that I'd previously marked page 317 with a green Post-It tab. (How careful of me. How librarian of me.) Poem 640, "I cannot live with You – ", is one of Dickinson's greatest poems. It takes up the entirety of page 317 and carries over to page 318. It's a poem I return to because it continues to fascinate me.

In the span of a few minutes, through a series of small, fortuitous occurrences, three Dickinson poems have become connected with one another in my mind. Constellated there, her poems and their patterns are the result of a trail that made itself known—a trail I didn't know I needed to follow, but one that I trusted.

Poetry has no proof nor plan nor evidence by decree or in any other way. From somewhere in the twilight realm of sound a spirit of belief flares up at the point where meaning stops and the unreality of what seems most real floods over us. The inward ardor I feel while working in research libraries is intuitive. It's a sense of self-identification and trust, or the granting of grace in an ordinary room, in a secular time. —Susan Howe[4]

As a collection development librarian who works in a university library, I'm constantly negotiating a realm of things that seem real—ebooks, use data, information stored in clouds—and a

---

3. Emily Dickinson, *The Collected Poems of Emily Dickinson*, edited by Thomas H. Johnson (New York: Back Bay Books/Little, Brown & Company, 1961).

4. Susan Howe, *Spontaneous Particulars: The Telepathy of the Archives* (New York: Christine Burgin/New Directions, 2014), 63.

realm of things that feel real, are right here with me: the book I'm holding, the map on the table, that painting on the wall. As a poet, I'm constantly aware of uncertainty; it rules and I follow. I can live with it. As a librarian, there are instances in which I can't live long with uncertainty; somebody needs something now, and I can help them find that something, configure that something, negotiate that something. There's a divide between not knowing and knowing, a tension I move with and through every day.

For a long time I wouldn't call myself a poet. I still have a hard time saying it. I think of William Carlos Williams saying he'd rather go off and die like a sick dog than be a well-known literary person in America. I think of Heather McHugh, the best teacher of writing I've had, saying, "My whole life feels like a blue streak issuing from a solitude."[5] I think of Joy Williams and her terrific "Uncanny the Singing that Comes from Certain Husks," in which she says, "Writers when they're writing live in a spooky, clamorous silence, a state somewhat like the advanced stages of prayer but without prayer's calming benefits."[6]

I don't hesitate to call myself a librarian. And yet I've been working at poetry much longer than I've been working at librarianship. Sometimes people cringe or roll their eyes when you bring up poetry. You're too precious. You're pretentious. Or poems are too difficult; they take time and nobody has any time. Or your writing doesn't say enough about you.

For what glimpses of me are you reading?

Why?

I don't write in order to be surveilled, though I want my writing to be read. (Surveillance is sinister.) I write in order to keep going, though most of the time I feel directionless. I write because there's always some word or sound or passage that begs attention,

5. Christine Hume, "A Singing Kind of Seeing: Heather McHugh and Christine Hume in Conversation," *Poets.org*, August 4, 2004, https://www.poets.org/poetsorg/text/singing-kind-seeing-heather-mchugh-and-christine-hume-conversation.

6. Joy Williams, "Uncanny the Singing that Comes from Certain Husks," accessed December 27, 2016, https://extensivereadinguae.files.wordpress.com/2013/12/16-uncanny-the-singing-that-comes-from-certain-husks.pdf.

demands concentration. I write because (and despite my minor, unoriginal complaints about the difficulty of writing) I need and like the process.

———

In his study of the stanza, Ernst Häublein says the word's Italian etymology ". . . implies that stanzas are subordinate units within the more comprehensive unity of the whole poem."[7] The meaning of stanza is "room." I picture Sappho's fragments, Wallace Stevens's tercets and quatrains, Marianne Moore's loping forms, Robert Creeley's elegant shapes. A reader learns a poet by the ways in which the poet negotiates space. Given enough time, that same reader comes to recognize the poet's hand, mind, and sound at work on the page. The reader is allowed into many rooms, so much so that a kind of dwelling becomes apparent, as in the last lines of Stevens's "Final Soliloquy of the Interior Paramour":[8]

> We make a dwelling in the evening air,
> In which being there together is enough.

The great Anne Carson carries this idea a step further when she says, "If prose is a house, poetry is a man on fire running quite fast through it."[9]

The ways in which I think about room as a poet are similar to the ways in which I think about room as a librarian. At its most simple, a library could be a room, or many rooms, full of materials. A container. When working at collection development and purchasing books, DVDs, musical scores, journals for the library, I have to consider another form of room: space. Is there enough of

---

7. Edward Hirsch, *A Poet's Glossary* (New York: Houghton Mifflin Harcourt, 2014), 608-609.

8. Wallace Stevens, *The Collected Poems of Wallace Stevens* (New York: Alfred A. Knopf, 1954).

9. Kate Kellaway, "Anne Carson: 'I Do Not Believe in Art as Therapy,'" The Guardian, October 30, 2016, accessed December 27, 2016, https://www.theguardian.com/books/2016/0ct/30/anne-carson-do-not-believe-art-therapy-interview-float.

it? When will we run out of it? Then there's the idea of space as it pertains to storage of electronic resources, remote hosting versus local hosting. How do we care for this non-tangible thing?

When I'm working on a poem, room is space, a container, the meadow to which Robert Duncan wrote of being permitted to return, breath. I've made notes from and about whatever I've read, heard, seen, felt; now to make the poem. When I begin, I have no end or specific subject in mind, but a musical passage or image that's hounding me. I start with a blank piece of paper, 8.5 x 11, and transfer words and phrases from my notebook to the paper. A list accrues, and certain phrases begin to sound interesting together, certain shapes begin to look interesting together. I concentrate on those sounds, place phrases together and take them apart, and at some point a stanza arrives. Later—how much later is hard to say—a poem forms.

It's rare for me to write a poem in one sitting. On the off chance a quick poem happens, I tend to doubt it. For me, writing has always been a long process of arranging and re-arranging, chipping away. I attribute my discipline (well, bouts of discipline, anyway) and concentration to classical piano lessons I started at four years old. For years, I practiced hours a day, learning how to hold and move my hands on the keyboard, listening to dynamics and phrase shapes, keeping time. I don't think it's a coincidence that, thirty years later, I find myself pulling disparate pieces of information together in order to build a library's collection or make a poem, or that I require a certain amount of solitude in order to operate among firm orders, license agreements, fiscal year budgets, proxy servers, trochees, spondees, dactyls, words.

For the record, I still play piano. Chopin's nocturnes, preludes, and waltzes have my heart.

Also, another name for stanza is stave, which is another name for staff: a set of five parallel lines and the spaces between them, the figure on which music is written.

To answer a question sometimes asked of me: no, there wasn't a specific occurrence that made me want to become a librarian. My grandmother was a librarian, my mother is a librarian, but nobody told me that librarianship was something I should consider. It took me twenty-five years to arrive at that idea myself, and another six years to go through school for library science and find a job as a librarian. It took me thirty-one years to get started, whatever started means in regard to a lifetime.

In the process of all that going through things, I was working on writing my first and second books of poems. I found the necessary time and space in Suzzallo Reading Room at the University of Washington, where I was in graduate school first for creative writing, then librarianship, and where I worked as an archives and reference assistant in Special Collections. The Suzzallo Reading Room is the only part of UW Libraries designated a silent study area. It's a magnificent, Collegiate Gothic room. It also happens to be in close proximity to the P stacks: language and literature. For a few hours most nights that's where I would be, moving between reading and writing, and hunting for books in the stacks.

I knew I would likely not be afforded that kind of space or unfettered time again, and I knew I had to act accordingly. The work I accomplished there changed my life. Two full-length collections of poems made their way out of that room, and my decision to seriously pursue librarianship took shape in that room. I discovered the work of poets whose writing I might have arrived at much later or not at all: Alan Dugan, whose *Poems*—a book that was once in the P stacks but has now been moved to the auxiliary stacks in Suzzallo—won the 1962 Pulitzer Prize for Poetry; and Laura Jensen, a Tacoma, Washington native whose poems are marvelous gems. I learned that I wanted to somehow cultivate and sustain that same sense of space for others, space to make sense of whatever is or isn't in front of you, space to move among materials that, at a certain juncture, might deliver to you something enduring.

Bibliography

Carr, Patrick L. "Serendipity in the Stacks: Libraries, Information Architecture, and the Problems of Accidental Discovery." *College & Research Libraries* 76, no. 6 (2015): 831-842. http://crl.acrl.org/content/early/2015/01/01/crl14-655. full.pdf+html.

Dickinson, Emily. *The Collected Poems of Emily Dickinson.* Edited by Thomas H. Johnson. New York: Back Bay Books/Little, Brown & Company, 1961.

Harvard University Press. "Emily Dickinson Archive." Accessed December 23, 2016. http://www.edickinson.org/.

Hirsch, Edward. *A Poet's Glossary.* New York: Houghton Mifflin Harcourt, 2014.

Howe, Susan. *Spontaneous Particulars: The Telepathy of the Archives.* New York: Christine Burgin/New Directions, 2014.

Hume, Christine. "A Singing Kind of Seeing: Heather McHugh and Christine Hume in Conversation." *Poets.org,* August 4, 2004. Accessed October 20, 2016. https://www.poets. org/poetsorg/text/singing-kind-seeing-heather-mchugh-and-christine-hume-conversation.

Kellaway, Kate. "Anne Carson: 'I Do Not Believe in Art as Therapy'." *The Guardian,* October 30, 2016. Accessed December 27, 2016. https://www.theguardian.com/ books/2016/oct/30/anne-carson-do-not-believe-art-therapy-interview-float.

Liestman, Daniel. "Chance in the Midst of Design: Approaches to Library Research Serendipity." *RQ* 31, no. 4 (1992): 524-532. http://www.jstor.org/stable/25829128.

McLane, Maureen. "Susan Howe, The Art of Poetry No. 97." *Paris Review*, Winter 2012. https://www.theparisreview. org/interviews/6189/susan-howe-the-art-of-poetry-no-97-susan-howe.

Ranganathan, S.R. *The Five Laws of Library Science*. London: Edward Goldston, Ltd., 1931.

"Room (v.); room (n.)." *Online Etymology Dictionary*. http://www. etymonline.com/.

Stevens, Wallace. *The Collected Poems of Wallace Stevens*. New York: Alfred A. Knopf, 1954.

Williams, Joy. "Uncanny the Singing that Comes from Certain Husks." Accessed December 27, 2016. https:// extensivereadinguae.files.wordpress.com/2013/12/16-uncanny-the-singing-that-comes-from-certain-husks.pdf.

Internal Voicemail Greeting

Shannon Tharp

Rare, the days
I'm talked with,
rather than at or to.

It seems I'm present
only to be
made use of.

Amid estimates
of attrition,
my body's

more shadow
than human, more money
than shadow.

It's impossible
to say where,
if anywhere,

I am. Which is
to say I'm
not available.

Chapter 14

'IN SILENCE, FOR SILENCE, OUT OF SILENCE':
A POET-LIBRARIAN ACTIVISM

Oliver Baez Bendorf

Lately I have been thinking about silence: moving through it, coming out of it, its appeals and its violences, and how this work converges at a natural overlap between "poet" and "librarian." Sooner or later any of us involved critically with either poetry or librarianship will bump up against this reckoning with silence; isn't silence fetishized, to a certain degree, by many of us? I am seeking a better understanding of the different ways that we can understand silence through both poetry and librarianship, and to trace its power, and so I have been asking these questions (borrowed after Barthes' questions on how meaning is made): silence for whom, by what means, and at what cost?[1]

I have been thinking about silence in relation to library work because libraries already are in the business of silence, whether or not we believe it to be political. A thread on Reddit from 2010 asks, "When and why did libraries stop being silent? Give me back

---

1. Roland Barthes, "The Structuralist Activity." in *Criticism: Major Statements*, 4th ed., edited by Charles Kaplan and William Anderson (New York: Macmillan, 1999).

my shushing librarians!"[2] But libraries were never silent in the natural order of things. Libraries were or are silent because library workers silenced. More popularly, they shushed. While many in the profession have critiqued and disavowed the stereotype of the disciplinarian, shushing librarian, perhaps we as a profession have not gone far enough to reflect on and repair our role in silencing, which exists on a spectrum and is hardly ever enforced equitably. Silencing involves power. Often, we internalize silencing messages, and silence ourselves. A poet silencing hir thoughts while staring at a blank page, for example, or a library worker afraid to speak out at a meeting. The poet Fred Moten writes about "the silencing of things, the silence of an unheard case, of a muffled appeal consigned to lower frequencies."[3]

I am thinking of Jordan Davis, a black seventeen-year-old boy who Michael Dunn shot and killed because he felt the music in Davis' car was too loud. Dunn told his wife "I hate that thug music" and proceeded to shoot Davis in the legs, lungs, and aorta, then went to his hotel and ordered pizza. They call the sound suppressor a "silencer" but isn't that, actually, what the entire gun is meant to be? In his writing on the fatal violence of our country's Jim Crow era, the poet Jake Adam York reminds us of the frequent collocation of silence and violence: "a young man's voice / becomes a young man's / silence."[4] After many readings of these same lines, I realize that even as York memorializes through lyric the taking away of a young man's voice, he insists that the silence still belongs to the same young man, even in his death. But is our silence ever ours?

Although often viewed as the shushers themselves, librarians have also been silenced, subject to policing of what they can and cannot tell the communities they serve—in the name of, no

2. Reddit, "When and why did libraries stop being silent? Give me back my shushing librarians!", 2010, https://www.reddit.com/r/books/comments/bbfk8/when_and_why_did_libraries_stop_being_silent_give/.

3. Fred Moten, "the plan," *Harriet the Blog*, The Poetry Foundation, January 10, 2010, https://www.poetryfoundation.org/harriet/2010/01/the-plan/.

4. Jake Adam York, "Mayflower," in *Abide* (Carbondale, IL: Southern Illinois University Press, 2014).

surprise, national security. In the years after the Patriot Act, the FBI served national security letters to librarians, forbidding them to disclose to anyone that the FBI sought or obtained access to library user's records, a silencing described in *Mother Jones* as a "lifetime gag order."[5]

While beautiful, transformative, necessary things can happen in quiet, I don't believe anything good ever happens in silence. But who can afford to speak out? The stakes for doing so are not equal for all of us. Emerging, POC, queer/trans, women, disabled, paraprofessional library and archive workers face more precarity and we all weigh how much we can say, when, and to whom.

I keep turning over in my mind that by now well-known passage from Audre Lorde, "My silences had not protected me. Your silence will not protect you."[6] I turn it around with the knowledge, comfort, and challenge that Audre Lorde was not only a poet and activist, but also a librarian (a little-known-fact that I thank my former professor Ethelene Whitmire for helping to gain wider traction). Lorde penned that essay while steeped in work as a librarian, poet, and activist in the civil rights, women's rights, and anti-war movements of the time, fifteen years after earning her master's degree in library science from Columbia. If silence itself can operate as a violent force, overcoming it often also necessitates force. "There are so many silences to be broken,"[7] she writes. I have wondered before about this word "break" and the multiple levels on which it operates. I have thought about it before in the context of poets "breaking" lines, deciding when and where to drop the next word to another line. The library field has paid much attention in recent years to "making" and its role in our work; it seems to

---

5. Amy Goodman and David Goodman, "America's Most Dangerous Librarians," *Mother Jones*, Sept/Oct, 2008, http://www.motherjones.com/politics/2008/09/americas-most-dangerous-librarians.

6. Audre Lorde, "The Transformation of Silence into Language and Action," in *Sister Outsider: Essays and Speeches* (Trumansburg, NY: Crossing Press, 1984), 41, https://www.csusm.edu/sjs/documents/silenceintoaction.pdf.

7. Ethelene Whitmire, "The Audre Lorde was a Librarian Project," http://theaudrelordelibrarianproject.blogspot.com/.

me now that "breaking" is just as much our work: barriers, yes, silences.

Still, silence is an ideal for which many long, and feel anxious and angry without. The poet Rae Armantrout lamented in 1985 the waning of "natural silence" in the world and praised poems in which silence operates as a "conscious component" of the aesthetic. But when, I wonder, was this "natural silence"? And who for, and at what cost, and by what means? Reading her essay, it seems to me that the "silence" she mourns in poetry is more like room for uncertainty, tolerance for ambiguity, waiting, and discomfort: her beef is with "a tone of certainty, of resolution and completeness which leaves little room for the experiences of silence."[8] I agree that the experience of uncertainty/ambiguity is useful to tolerate and even cultivate; in poetry, in library work, in activism. This "silence" can feel unnatural. After a recent writing and drawing workshop I taught in my living room, one participant confessed to me her own discomfort, at first, with moments of quiet during instruction. "Why isn't he saying anything?" she recalled thinking, before realizing that I intended for these moments to be there, as a kind of holding space. "There are so many different ways to be silent,"[9] the poet Kazim Ali reminds us. This kind of silence, a comfort with gaps between language and action, did not come naturally to me when I first began to teach. This kind of silence is an invitation toward disclosure—"I am willing to wait for what you want to say"—and a way to create the conditions for discovery. Both libraries and poetry offer discovery, which I think is what Armantrout was after when she bemoaned the lack of silence. It's about holding a space that neither answer nor narrative can fill...holding a space for more questions. Besides, as Chris Bourg reminds us, "serendipity is fun,"[10] and this too is the work of libraries, through browsing and discovery.

---

8. Rae Armantrout, "Poetic Silence," In *Writing/Talks*, ed. Bob Perelman (Carbondale, IL: Southern Illinois University Press, 1985): 41.

9. Kazim Ali, "Faith and Silence," *American Poetry Review* 26, no. 6 (Nov/Dec, 2007): 10.

10. Chris Bourg, "lots of folks like to discover," *Feral Librarian*, July 26, 2016, https://chris.wordpress.com/2016/07/26/lots-of-folks-like-to-discover/.

My own relationship to silence has been shaped by the literal transformation of my own voice since beginning testosterone therapy in January 2013 as a transgender man. Like a second puberty, but in adulthood, my voice cracked unpredictably, without care for whether I was in the middle of teaching a room full of freshmen, or reading a draft of a poem aloud in workshop, or on the phone ordering pizza. When shame lives in silence, what is one to do when the very tool they use to break that silence—their voice—is erratic, embarrassing, yes, shameful? One answer is to write. Another: grow comfortable with the discomfort. I did both of those things, plus a third: I took voice lessons. Not for speaking, but for singing. My relationship to silence has been shaped by the social transformation of my presence in the room to that of someone who is read as a man. I am interrupted less, shushed less, silenced less, and in continual reflection on how to use my voice (now a man's) responsibly, and when to be quiet. It has been illuminating to see ways that silence is inequitably distributed across gender. For me, staying committed to using my voice through its cracks and awkward public transformation has been not only personal, but also political; I see it as part of a continual process of divesting from shame. Ali, in reflecting on prayer, writes about his "shame at keeping silent, at wanting that silence to be beautiful. Silence wrote back as poems."[11] His longing for silence to be beautiful: I can relate. And can't it be? Or is it only quiet that can be beautiful? Is silence always a perpetuation of violence and shame?

"What I most regretted were my silences," Lorde reflects in her essay,[12] which began as a paper delivered at the Modern Language Association's "Lesbian and Literature" panel in Chicago in 1977. When I was in high school, I quietly sat out from observing the National Day of Silence, meant to draw attention to harmful silencing of LGBTQ youth. My non-participation confused people, as I was a visible and open LGBTQ youth myself. But I felt, and I remember trying to articulate, that the only way out of silence

---

11. Ali, "Faith and Silence," 8.

12. Lorde, "The Transformation of Silence," 41.

was through speech, not more silence, even if that silence was a performative political act. I know now that there is more nuance than this. But it remains true that the silence of marginalized people is often politically convenient, and so withdrawing our speech can only help do that work for us. (A labor strike, on the other hand . . .) It takes a squeak out of a machine. And a machine needs all the squeaks that we who dissent can muster. We cannot repair silence with more silence. Speaking truth to power is never without risk, but the time has come when the risk of staying silent is even greater.

Poetry can help us understand different kinds of silences in library work. What kind of silence is an archival silence? Is it a caesura, which falls outside the meter (established rhythm) for a poem, and thus can sometimes go unnoticed? Or is it a metrical silence, which takes the place of speech within the established rhythm and thus is easier to notice? There are many activists in our field helping to shift archival silences from the realm of barely-there caesuras into the realm of gaping metrical silences, and this is necessary work that comes from establishing a framework by which to notice them. Similarly, we can shift all-white and all-male panels and staffs, from the realm of invisible caesuras to the realm of metrical silences we cannot ignore, by training ourselves to look for whose voices are missing, and by extension, what silence is being perpetuated. What are the silences enabled and reinforced by diversity and inclusion measures? How do we go beyond that?

In my own work to organize librarians, writers, and artists, I have found this to be a powerful and symbiotic coalition for advocacy, public art, information literacy, social action, prison activism, community organizing, and DIY publishing. Thousands of librarians, writers, and artists spoke out together, along with students, editors, and social workers, against the publication of a dehumanizing anti-trans essay in the *Antioch Review*.[13] Hundreds of librarians, LGBTQ and people of color

13. *"Antioch Review*: No More Transphobia in the Literary Community," May 4, 2016, https://docs.google.com/document/d/1Pa55lmSxJ-SSgdpqS9s 8dJuwOA64J-eUaozbmxocgww/edit.

activists, and writers contributed resources and organization to the #PulseOrlandoSyllabus in the aftermath of that violence. And when dozens of transgender writers came together on Twitter for the first intentional #translit chat, librarians quietly observed and listened, helped spread the word, and took note of information needs expressed by participants.

When Lorde told her daughter that she was writing on silence and struggling with it, her daughter replied, "Tell them about how you're never really a whole person if you remain silent, because there's always that one little piece inside you that wants to be spoken out, and if you keep ignoring it, it gets madder and madder and hotter and hotter, and if you don't speak it out one day it will just up and punch you in the mouth from the inside."[14] As a trans person, I feel that my whole life is on a careening track toward becoming more whole; it is exhausting and often inconvenient, but Lorde's daughter was right about the alternative. I am inspired by the work of librarians and archivists around me to create more openness in our field, in a number of ways: to create spaces for things to be said, and to help those things to reach more people. And I am carried by the work of fellow poets dedicated to making necessary art in these times of racial injustice, police brutality, Islamophobia, and policing of transgender bodies; those who "refuse to be timid," per the call from Dark Noise Collective.[15]

Silence is a thread that stitches together systems of injustice. It is also a state for which at least some of our library users long, a condition at least some poets require for writing, and an ideal that John Cage reminds us never really existed. Maybe the loudness we so desire to escape stems not only from the outside, but also from those "little pieces" inside us that want to be spoken out, that have grown noisier in our neglect.

---

14. Lorde, "The Transformation of Silence," 42.

15. Dark Noise Collective, "A Call for Necessary Craft and Practice," 2016, https://docs.google.com/document/d/1mLGU7jtAPL9JHuNX0Vz9hHdvnhif OLui8ZzqEymh03A/edit.

Bibliography

Ali, Kazim. "Faith and Silence." *American Poetry Review* 36, no. 6 (Nov/Dec 2007: 7-11.

"*Antioch Review:* No More Transphobia in the Literary Community." May 4, 2016. https://docs.google.com/ document/d/1Pa55lmSxJ-SSgdpqS9s8dJuwOA64J- eUaozbmxocgww/edit.

Armantrout, Rae. "Poetic Silence." In *Writing/Talks*, edited by Bob Perelman. Carbondale, IL: Southern Illinois University Press, 1985.

Barthes, Roland. "The Structuralist Activity." In *Criticism: Major Statements*, 4th ed., edited by Charles Kaplan and William Anderson, 487–92. New York: Macmillan, 1999.

Bourg, Chris. "lots of folks like to discover." *Feral Librarian.* July 26, 2016. https://chrisbourg.wordpress.com/2016/07/26/ lots-of-folks-like-to-discover/.

Cage, John. *Silence.* Hanover, NH: Wesleyan University Press, 1973.

Dark Noise Collective. "A Call for Necessary Craft and Practice." 2016. https://docs.google.com/document/d/1mLGU7jtA PL9JHuNX0Vz9hHdvnhifOLui8ZzqEymh03A/edit.

Goodman, Amy, and David Goodman. "America's Most Dangerous Librarians." *Mother Jones*, Sept/Oct, 2008. http://www.motherjones.com/politics/2008/09/ americas-most-dangerous-librarians.

Lorde, Audre. "The Transformation of Silence into Language and Action." In *Sister Outsider: Essays and Speeches*, 40-44. Trumansburg, NY: Crossing Press, 1984. https://www. csusm.edu/sjs/documents/silenceintoaction.pdf.

Moten, Fred. "the plan." *Harriet the Blog.* The Poetry Foundation. January 10, 2010. https://www.poetryfoundation.org/harriet/2010/01/the-plan/.

#PulseOrlandoSyllabus. 2016. Edited by Oliver Baez Bendorf, Jamie Berrout, Venus Selenite, Lydia Willoughby. bit.ly/orlandosyllabus.

Reddit. "When and why did libraries stop being silent? Give me back my shushing librarians!" 2010. https://www.reddit.com/r/books/comments/bbfk8 /when_and_why_did_libraries_stop_being_silent_give/.

#translit Twitter chat. 2016. https://storify.com/ohbendorf/translit-twitter-chat.

Whitmire, Ethelene. "The Audre Lorde was a Librarian Project." http://theaudrelordelibrarianproject.blogspot.com/

York, Jake Adam. "Mayflower." In *Abide.* Carbondale, IL: Southern Illinois University Press, 2014.

Take Care

Oliver Baez Bendorf

Sometimes I mistake the sound of my voice
for a rubber tire on the shoulder of the road.
I mistake my shoulder for an angle formed
by two lines coming together in geometry.
I mistake my geometry for the way mothers
are the holy holy holiest of holes in the heart
and I mistake my holy for a dried up plant
rolled into the pages of someone else's vision.
I am just as full of shit as everyone, incl. you.
And I mistake my fullness for abeyance,
mistake suspension for an early spring
rabbit hiding frozen in the road—I am
not the spring rabbit, I know, but it's easy
to mistake my ears for tambourines; I am
good at them without expending any effort.
Once I mistook the tart infatuation of a
kumquat for another seedless calamity.
I mistake seeds for nothing all the time.
I mistake time for space, space for freedom,
sparkles in the alley for a sign that our
universe is sentient after all, and loving,
and will take care of those of us who pray
however mistakenly, not on our knees
exactly, but with our hands clasped
that we may be mistaken for believers.
I mistake my hands for belief all the time.
I keep waking up expecting them to be
someone else's, but so far they're only
mine, and when I mistake distance for
absence I tend to go astray. Like when
I can't tell if someone is walking away

from me or toward me until it's too late
in either direction. I wonder whether coroners
mistake knees for elbows the way my love
loses track of left and right. There are times,
or should I say spaces, in which I mistake
fire for work gloves, which is almost always
a mistake and vice versa. I want a compass.
I need deliverance. Good god, take me,
mistake me back to the soft shoulder,
which I mistake so often for the road itself.

[From *The Spectral Wilderness* (Kent State University Press, 2015); first published in *jubilat*].

About the Contributors

Oliver Baez Bendorf is the 2017-2018 Halls Emerging Artist Fellow at the Wisconsin Institute for Creative Writing. His first poetry collection, *The Spectral Wilderness* (Kent State University, 2015), was selected by Mark Doty for the Wick Poetry Prize and named a finalist for the Thom Gunn Award for Gay Poetry. His writing has also appeared in *Alaska Quarterly Review*, *The Feminist Wire*, *Indiana Review*, *Transgender Studies Quarterly*, *Troubling the Line: Trans and Genderqueer Poetry and Poetics*, and elsewhere. He is a co-editor of the #PulseOrlandoSyllabus. He has received fellowships from the Lambda Literary Foundation, Vermont Studio Center, and University of Wisconsin-Madison, where he earned an MFA in Poetry and an MLIS, and where he currently teaches creative writing and queer poetics.

Sommer Browning is Associate Director of Technical and Financial Services at Auraria Library, a library that serves University of Colorado, Denver, Metropolitan State University of Denver, and Community College of Denver. She received her MFA in poetry from the University of Arizona and an MSLIS from Long Island University. She is the author of *Either Way I'm Celebrating* (Birds, LLC; 2011), a collection of poetry and comics; *Backup Singers* (Birds, LLC; 2014), a collection of poetry; *The Circle Book* (Cuneiform, 2015), an artist book; and most recently *Want to Hear About This Dream I Had* (Reality Beach, 2016), a collection of dreams. She lives in Denver where she co-hosts Death Horse, a reading series.

Yago S. Cura is a Bilingual Community Outreach Librarian for the Los Angeles Public Library. He is proprietor of HINCHAS

Press, which published *Librarians with Spines: Information Agitators in an Age of Stagnation* in 2017. "Hoisting the Disenfranchised..." was written during a period when Yago was the Adult Services Librarian at the Vernon Branch. Yago is a former N.Y.C. Teaching Fellow and A.L.A. Spectrum Scholar. Along with Ryan Nance, he is the co-founder of the Copa Poetica (http://copapoetica.us), a three day reading series in Los Angeles that transpired on the rest days of the 2014 World Cup. His Spanglish blog, Spicaresque (http://spicaresque.blogspot.com), has had more than 64,000 visitors. Yago's poetry has appeared in *Acentos Review, Huizache, KWELI, PALABRA, Borderlands, Lungfull!, COMBO, LIT, U.S. Latino Review, 2nd Avenue, Exquisite Corpse, FIELD*, and *Slope*. His reviews have appeared in *The St.Mark's Poetry Project Newsletter*. He is currently translating Facundo Soto's "Juego de chicos: Crònicas de fútbol gay" for the English language fiction market

Melissa Eleftherion is a writer, librarian, and a visual artist. She grew up in Brooklyn, dropped out of high school, and went on to earn an MFA in Poetry from Mills College and an MLIS from San Jose State University. She is the author of six chapbooks: *huminsect, prism maps, Pigtail Duty, the leaves the leaves, abalone, & green glass asterisms*. Her first full-length collection, *field guide to autobiography*, was published by H_NGM_N in April 2017. Founder of the Poetry Center Chapbook Exchange for San Francisco State University, Melissa now lives in Mendocino County where she works as a Teen Librarian, teaches creative writing, & curates the LOBA Reading Series at Ukiah Library

Marie Elia is the Processing Archivist for the Poetry Collection of the University Libraries at the University at Buffalo. She received her MLIS from the University of Pittsburgh and MFA in Creative Writing from Columbia University. Her chapbook *Girlhood and Machines* was published by Dancing Girl Press in 2015. She is an editor of *The Reading Room: A Journal of Special Collections*.

Michalle Gould's first full-length collection of poetry, *Resurrection Party*, was published by Silver Birch Press in 2014 and was a finalist for the Writers League of Texas Book Award in poetry. Her work has appeared in *Poetry*, *Slate*, *New England Review*, *The Texas Observer*, *The Toast*, *The Nervous Breakdown*, *The Awl*, and others. Her poem "How Not To Need Resurrection" was adapted into a short film for the Motionpoems webseries (www.motionpoems.com), and other work has been set to music by the founder of the Washington Women in Jazz Festival. She currently lives in Hollywood, where she works as an academic librarian at the Art Institute of California-Hollywood. In her free time she's learning to play the accordion, collaborating on an opera, and writing a novel set in the north of England in the 1930s.

Sam Lohmann works as a reference librarian at Washington State University, Vancouver. He is the author of several books and chapbooks, including *Stand on this picnic bench and look north* (Publication Studio, 2011), *Unless As Stone Is* (eth press, 2014) and *Day Use Area* (Couch Press, 2014). He's one of the organizers of the Spare Room reading series in Portland, Oregon, and co-edits Airfoil Chapbooks with David Abel. From 2006 until 2013, he edited the handmade poetry fanzine *Peaches and Bats*.

Aaron McCollough lives in Washington, D.C. His most recent poetry collections include *Rank* (University of Iowa Press, 2015), *Underlight* (Ugly Duckling Presse, 2012), and *No Grave Can Hold My Body Down* (Ahsahta Press, 2011). He has worked as a librarian at the University of Michigan and the University of Illinois.

Edric Mesmer serves as cataloger to the Poetry Collection of the University Libraries, University at Buffalo. Additionally, he serves as collator of the small & stapled journal of poetry *Yellow Field* and the Buffalo Ochre Papers series of chapettes. His poetry collection *of monodies and homophony* won the Outriders Poetry Project prize for 2014. The poem "Clauses escaping from within archival asylum as breath" first appeared in the privately printed chapbook *Don't Let's* (2016).

Michele R. Santamaría is the Learning Design Librarian at Millersville University. She was born in Quito, Ecuador and grew up in Miami, Florida. Before landing in Millersville, Pennsylvania, Michele lived and studied in St. Andrews, Scotland; Eugene, Oregon; and Manhattan. In 2016, Michele co-authored a book chapter for ACRL's *Metaliteracy in Practice*, which focused on students' efforts to be self-reflective about their research by examining the way they analyzed their own metacognitive processes. In her 2017 book chapter in ACRL's *The Self as Subject: Autoethnographic Research into Identity, Culture, and Academic Librarianship*, Michele reflected upon her life experiences and combined a creative non-fiction approach with research on silence, libraries, immigration, and noise sensitivity. Michele is also the English librarian at Millersville University and welcomes all kinds of conversations about teaching and learning. Michele tweets at @MUEngLib.

Jessica Smith, Founding Editor of *Foursquare* and *name* magazines and Coven Press, is a librarian in Alabama. She is the author of numerous chapbooks including *Trauma Mouth* (dusie) and two full-length books, *Organic Furniture Cellar* (Outside Voices) and *Life-List* (Chax Press).

Shannon Tharp is Collections & Content Management Librarian at the University of Denver's Anderson Academic Commons. She received her MFA in Creative Writing and her MLIS from the University of Washington. She is the author of the chapbooks *Each Real Bird* (Elliott Press), *Determined by Aperture* (Fewer & Further), *Quarry* (Calaveras), and the full-length collections *The Cost of Walking* (Skysill Press) and *Vertigo in Spring* (The Cultural Society). She lives in Denver.

Itza Vilaboy is a Library and Information Technology student at Palomar College in San Marcos, CA, where her goal is to become a Librarian. She is a Library Intern at Museum of Contemporary Art San Diego; San Diego County Library, Solana Beach Branch; San Diego Public Library, Central; and San Diego City College Library/Learning Resource Center. Her work has been featured at *Open Space*, Los Angeles (2016), Light & Wire Gallery, and in other arts publications. She lives in Southern California.

Patrick Williams is Associate Librarian for Literature, Rhetoric, and Digital Humanities in the Syracuse University Libraries. He studies past, present, and future technologies of reading and writing. Patrick holds a B.A. in English from The University of North Carolina at Greensboro and an M.S. and Ph.D. in Information Studies from The University of Texas at Austin. He was a 2015 Techpaths Fellow and visiting artist at Wheaton College in Massachusetts. His research and writing appears in the *Critical Library Pedagogy Handbook*, the *Journal of Academic Librarianship*, the *Canadian Journal of Information and Library Science*, *Heavy Feather Review*, *Posit*, *Glittermobs*, and elsewhere. His poetry chapbook *Hygiene in Reading* (Publishing Genius, 2016) was awarded the 2015 Chris Toll Memorial Prize. He is lead editor of The *dh+lib Review* and founder and editor of *Really System*, a journal of poetry and extensible poetics.

Scott Woods is the author of *Urban Contemporary History Month* and *We Over Here Now* (2016 and 2013, Brick Cave Books), and has published and edited work in a variety of publications. He has been featured in national press, including appearances on National Public Radio and in *Paste* magazine. He was the President of Poetry Slam Inc. and emcees the Writers' Block Poetry Night, an open mic series in Columbus, Ohio. In April 2006 he became the first poet to ever complete a 24-hour solo poetry reading, a feat he bested with seven more annual readings without repeating a single poem. He is a Customer Service Specialist II in the Columbus Metropolitan Library system, where he's worked for over twenty years—more than half of that time at the main library and the rest of it in an urban neighborhood branch library. He oversees the training of public services staff and works with customers in public service. More of his work can be found at www.scottwoodswrites.net.

INDEX